COLOSSIANS

A New Testament Commentary

Bob Yandian

√ 4/22 - 4/28 chpt 1
√ 4/29 5/5 chpt 2
√ 5/6 - 5/12 chpt 3
5/13 5/19 chpt 4

COLOSSIANS: A New Testament Commentary

ISBN: 978-1-68031-082-5
© 2016 by Bob Yandian
Bob Yandian Ministries
PO Box 55236
Tulsa, OK 74155
www.bobyandian.com

Published by Harrison House Publishers
Tulsa, OK 74155
www.harrisonhouse.com

19 18 17 16   10 9 8 7 6 5 4 3 2 1

Printed in the United States of America.

Table of Contents

COLOSSIANS

VERSE BY VERSE COMMENTARY

The personal study notes of BOB YANDIAN

Introduction

My heart echoes a statement Peter made in his last epistle:

For this reason I will not be negligent to remind you always of these things, though you know and are established in the present truth.

2 Peter 1:12

The "for this reason" was to build on his previous statement — Peter's desire for all believers not just to get to heaven but to have an abundant entrance into heaven. A working knowledge and practice of the Word of God is necessary for an abundant entrance, which is marked by rewards and rulership.

In order to establish that abundant entrance, Peter taught believers what they should know again and again, "though you know them." What was taught them was the present truth. The present truth is what was being written in the day of the apostles Peter, Paul, John, and James.

This present truth is what believers still need to be gloriously saved. The Old Testament is to be studied in the light of the New Testament epistles. The four gospels are to be studied in the light of the New Testament epistles. Not only should every Christian know the epistles, they should be established in them.

This is why I have written this series of books, verse-by-verse teachings on the epistles of Paul, Peter, John, and James. This is truly meat for our time period, our dispensation: the church age.

Bob Yandian
Author

Colossians Overview

Writer: The Apostle Paul.

Time: About 60–61 AD.

Occasion: The book of Colossians was written during Paul's first imprisonment in Rome (Ephesians 3:1, 4:1; Philippians 1:7, Colossians 4:18). It was during this same imprisonment that Paul wrote the epistles of Ephesians, Philippians, and Philemon. Ephesians and Colossians are parallel or "sister" books. They are two of the most concentrated because of the opposition of human philosophy challenging the Colossian church.

Paul wrote to the saints at Colosse because the false religion of Gnosticism had entered the church. He also wanted to firmly establish his support of Epaphras as pastor and head of the local church. Paul gives his "stamp of approval" to the ministry of Epaphras in two passages, found in the opening and closing of the epistle (1:7–8, 4:12–13).

Recipients: The residents of the Lycus Valley, located in the region of Phyrgia, which consisted of three cities: Colosse, Hierpolis, and Laodicea (4:13).

Theme: The person of the resurrected Jesus Christ as head of the Church — as the Son of God, and as the Savior of the Body — and the believer's identification with Christ in His death, burial, and resurrection.

Background on Colosse

The city of Colosse was located in a very wealthy area in the region of Phyrgia. There were three cities that worked together in the areas of business, commerce, and trade: Laodocia, Hierpolis, and Colosse. Much of the wealth of the area came from wool. In the church at Colosse a schism began to develop between the shepherds, who were generally uneducated and not wealthy, and businessmen, who were educated and very wealthy. The caste system that existed outside the church began to be an influence inside the church. When Gnosticism was introduced, it appealed to the more educated members of the church at Colosse.

Historical Background

On his second missionary journey, Paul took Silas with him to spread the gospel in the area of Phyrgia: "Now when they had gone throughout Phyrgia and the region of Galatia . . . " (Acts 16:6).

On his third missionary journey, Paul went back to the area of Phyrgia: "And after he had spent some time there, he departed, and went over all the country of Galatia and Phyrgia in order, strengthening all the disciples." (Acts 18:23).

Paul had never visited Colosse, nor did he personally establish the Colossian church. In essence, Paul was a "grandfather" to the church at Colosse.

In his letter, Paul was refuting Gnosticism, a false religion that combined doctrines from three different belief systems: Greek philosophy, legalistic Judaism, and Oriental dualism.

1:1–29 Christ Is Supreme

Challenge of Chapter One

Christians are to grow and apply the revelation knowledge of God's will and produce fruit in their daily lives. God's desire is that they walk through trials with patience, which strengthen them and cause them to be the encouragement and witness to the world.

Christ is the visible image of God, Who is invisible, and He created everything in both heaven and earth. It is through Him that all things created are held together. We are the body of Christ and He is the Head of the Church. We were once separated from God, but through the shed blood of Jesus, we have been reconciled to Him. We are admonished to continue in the truth of the Word because it is through the Word operating in our lives that we have hope for the future

I. Paul's Greeting to the Colossian Saints (1–2)

Paul affirms his call as an apostle and addresses both the saints and the faithful brethren.

A. Paul, an Apostle Called by God

1:1 ¶ Paul, an apostle of Jesus Christ by the will of God, and Timothy our brother,

Paul, an apostle (*apostolos*: sent one) of Jesus Christ by the will of God . . .

Paul, by birth, is a Jew from the tribe of Benjamin. By citizenship, he is Roman. But more importantly, in all of the epistles, Paul is identified as an apostle by the will of God; he is never said to be chosen of men.

1. Apostleship is a Ministry Gift

Apostleship is a spiritual ministry gift given by God (1 Corinthians 12:28; Ephesians 4:11, 13). The call to be an apostle is a matter of grace and therefore, it is in contrast to a talent (natural human ability from natural birth).

2. Church Apostles Appointed after the Resurrection

It isn't until after the resurrection of Christ that the apostles to the church are appointed(Ephesians 4:8, 11). The apostles to Israel (Matthew 10:1–6) are not the same as the apostles to the church.

3. An Apostle's Authority

An apostle exercises authority over all the churches that apostle has founded (e.g., Colosse, Ephesus, Jerusalem, etc.).

4. Apostles Today

Today apostles are still sent, but they have much less authority. They still establish churches but do not write scripture. (The Word of God is already complete.)

5. Apostolic Gifts

The office of the apostle is accompanied by spiritual gifts like the word of wisdom and the gifts of healing (1 Corinthians 12:8–11, Romans 11:29).

6. Apostles Called by God, Not Man

The story of Matthias in Acts 1:23–26 illustrates the futility of men trying to elect a minister. No person can elect people to spiritual offices or give spiritual gifts. Paul probably replaces Judas (1 Timothy 1:12–16, 1 Corinthians 15:7–10), yet he is not chosen by men or the original 12 disciples.

7. Early Apostles

Other than Paul, several men are delegated authority for apostleship including Barnabas (Acts 14:14), James (Galatians 1:19, 1 Corinthians 15:7), Apollos (1 Corinthians 4:6, 9), Sylvanus, and Timothy (1 Thessalonians 1:1, 2:6).

. . . and Timotheus (Timothy) our brother,

Timotheus is Timothy who worked with Paul and became the spiritual leader of the church at Ephesus.

B. Two Categories of Believers

1:2 To the saints and faithful brethren in Christ *who are* in Colosse: ¶ Grace to you and peace from God our Father and the Lord Jesus Christ.

To the saints . . .

1. Saints

A "saint" is a convert who attends church but is not committed to the church and is not growing in faith.

. . . and faithful brethren in Christ which are at Colosse . . .

2. Faithful Brethren

The "faithful brethren"are believers committed to serving God who are growing in faith. These people are disciples rather than converts (Psalm 111:1, Ephesians 1:1).

Both types of believers existed in the church at Colosse and still exist in the church today.

C. Grace and Peace from God

. . . Grace be unto you, and peace, from God our Father and the Lord Jesus Christ.

Grace always precedes peace. The greater the revelation of grace, the more peace becomes a controlling part of our lives and both grace and peace come from God the Father and the Lord Jesus Christ. Both can increase through knowledge of the Word of God (2 Peter 1:2). Some in the church at Colosse were cutting themselves off from the grace and peace of God by becoming involved in Gnosticism.

II. Paul's Thanksgiving and Prayer (3–14)

Although Paul had never met the believers at Colosse, we find in this section of scripture that he prays fervently for them. Paul also highly commends Epaphras as a faithful minister and pastor of the church at Colosse and not only makes reference to the inheritance of the saints, but also to the redemption that belongs to every born-again believer.

A. Paul's Thankfulness

1:3 ¶ We give thanks to the God and Father of our Lord Jesus Christ, praying always for you,

We give thanks (*eucharisteo*: to be grateful or to express gratitude) to God ("and" does not exist in the Greek) the father of our Lord Jesus Christ . . .

All thanks go to the Father (John 16:23).

B. Paul's Prayer for the Colossians

. . . praying (*proseuchomai*: face to face petition) always (*pantote*: at all times) for you,

Paul is praying face-to-face with God for people he does not know. This would involve praying in tongues as well as with the understanding. Praying for those we do not know is a very pure form of intercession.

1:4 since we heard of your faith in Christ Jesus and of your love for all the saints;

Since we heard of your faith in Christ Jesus (salvation) and the love (*agape*: divine love from the Holy Spirit) which you have for all the saints,

Paul prays for the saints and faithful members of the congregation when he hears of their salvation and spiritual growth. Their spiritual growth comes through the teaching of their pastor, Epaphras (1:7–8). Their love has grown to the point where they now love all saints, whether good or bad. This is the type of love that does not judge by the way it is treated but loves through the Holy Spirit and the new nature.

Paul begins his intense prayer for them when they are walking in love toward all saints. Usually, this would be the time most Christians would stop in their prayer lives and instead pray for other believers who have visible needs. But Paul knows that spiritual growth brings supernatural spiritual attacks. Believers need the greatest amount of spiritual help and strength from other members of the body of Christ during this time. Paul prays for the saints at Colosse and, through his prayer, upholds their arms in the battle they face.

1:5 because of the hope which is laid up for you in heaven, of which you heard before in the word of the truth of the gospel,

For (because of) the hope (*elpis*: assurance, confidence) which is laid up for you in heaven . . .

The reason the Colossian saints are growing in love and have hope is because the Word was being taught. The believers had faith in Christ, love toward all believers, and now, an assurance of a home in heaven. They operate in the best of life and eternity. We have an abundant life on earth and a greater life yet in heaven (Philippians 1:21).

. . . whereof (which) you previously heard (learned) before in the word of truth in the gospel;

All of the knowledge the Colossian saints have received — the new birth, the operation of love (4), and the assurance of eternity (5) — came from the Word of God beginning with the gospel. The Word saves, brings development and maturity, and gives hope for the future. The Word is our past, present, and future in the Christian life.

> **1:6 which has come to you, as *it has* also in all the world, and is bringing forth fruit, as *it is* also among you since the day you heard and knew the grace of God in truth;**

Which is come unto you, (being present in your midst) as it is in all the world . . .

The gospel has come to Colosse through those who heard Paul. The gospel not only had come to them, but had also infiltrated the cities and villages in the entire known world. By this time, the gospel has been taken to those who have never heard and was being received by many.

. . . and bringeth forth fruit, (and increases) as it doth also in you, since the day ye heard of it, and knew (*epiginosko*: understood, was revealed) the grace of God in truth.

From the day the gospel was presented to the Colossian people, they have been learning of God's grace. This is why their lives are growing and producing so rapidly. The heresy they are hearing will later be taken care of and their lives would again return to stability because of the grace which they know. Grace is a great stabilizer in our lives. The knowledge of grace they possess is a great tribute to their pastor who helps them maintain the grace they began with.

A number of the key members of the Colossian church have heard the gospel preached in Phyrgia during Paul's second and third missionary journeys and have taken the gospel back to their city. Paul meets those involved in starting the church at Colosse. One such important man is Epaphras.

C. The Pastor of Colosse

1:7 as you also learned from Epaphras, our dear fellow servant, who is a faithful minister of Christ on your behalf,

As (even as) ye also learned (*manthano*: comprehend) of (from) Epaphras our dear fellowservant (*sundoulos*: servant with the same master); who is (keeps on being) for you (on your behalf) a faithful minister (*diakonos*: teacher and pastor; servant, deacon, minister) of Christ.

Verse 7 introduces us to the pastor at Colosse: Epaphras. He was apparently from the city of Colosse and from the local congregation (4:12–13). He came through the ranks and became pastor of the church.

Epaphras does not become weary in well doing. He plods on, day by day, instructing his congregation in the Word of God. Not only is he faithful as the pastor, he is also a man of prayer. It is Epaphras who visited Paul in prison to report the opposition the Colossian church is facing. Paul's letter to the Colossians is a response to that report.

1. Epaphras

 a) A Fellow Servant

 Although Epaphras probably did not travel with Paul, Paul refers to him as a fellow servant and identifies him as part of his spiritual team.

 b) The Message of Grace

 Epaphras teaches his congregation about the grace of God (1:7). Grace is his main message. Epaphras has learned the Word under Paul and wants to remain on the same foundation he began with.

2. Faithful

Epaphras is called "faithful" (1:7) which is the highest commendation that can be given to a minister (1:2, 1 Timothy 1:12). Although Epaphras is not well known like Peter and others, God saw his faithfulness, and he was commended for it. His faithfulness included all areas of the ministry: study, prayer, worship, teaching, and the care of the congregation.

 a) Problems Not His Focus

 Epaphras reports to Paul the love of the people and their spirituality despite the problems which have occurred (1:8). He keeps his eyes on the spiritual attributes of the people rather than on the problems. Although problems exist and Epaphras knows it, he chooses to occupy himself with the majority of people who are following the Lord and growing in the Word.

b) From Colosse

Epaphras is apparently from the city of Colosse and from the local congregation (4:12). He came up through the ranks and became pastor of the church.

c) Man of Prayer

Epaphras prays earnestly for his congregation (4:12) and is interested in their welfare above his own.

d) Goal of Spiritual Maturity

His goal in prayer and in the ministry is for the congregation to become mature in all of the will of God (4:12). His desire is for the church at Colosse to be a spiritually mature congregation, unmovable in every area of their Christian lives. This means he has to teach on every area of the Word of God and not be afraid to venture into new areas of the Word.

e) His Vision

Epaphras is filled with great enthusiasm for the work of the ministry in his own city of Colosse, and he also has a vision and heart for the entire area of the Lycus Valley (4:13).

1:8 who also declared to us your love in the Spirit.

Who (Epaphras) also declared unto us your love (*agape*) in the Spirit.

Epaphras is quick to tell Paul of the maturity in the congregation despite the trouble in the church. He does not dwell on the isolated problem. The majority of the congregation was walking in love and in the Spirit. Those who were walking in the Spirit were producing fruit (Galatians 5:16), developing spiritual character, and maintaining stability.

D. Paul's Desire for the Colossian Saints

1:9 ¶ For this reason we also, since the day we heard it, do not cease to pray for you, and to ask that you may be filled with the knowledge of His will in all wisdom and spiritual understanding;

For this cause we also, since the day we heard it, do not cease to pray (*proseuchomai*: intense prayer) for you, and to desire (*epizeteo*: keep on asking) that ye might be filled (aorist passive subjunctive: receive filling) with the knowledge (*epignosis*: revelation knowledge from the Holy Spirit, not a natural knowledge) of his will . . .

Paul's prayer for the saints at Colosse is the same prayer that Epaphras prayed (4:12–13). Paul does not pray for his preaching to be great or to walk in a great anointing. Instead he prays for people to grow in the Word being taught and ministered to them. Revelation knowledge of the Word brings stability in the Christian life.

. . . in all wisdom (*sophia*: wisdom from the Word) and spiritual understanding.

Once the Word is learned, it must be applied against the circumstances of life. This is the production of wisdom. Wisdom is the correct application of knowledge (Proverbs 4:5–9).

E. A Fruitful Life

1:10 that you may walk worthy of the Lord, fully pleasing *Him*, being fruitful in every good work and increasing in the knowledge of God;

(In order) [t]hat ye might walk (*peripateo*: forward movement a step at a time) worthy (*axios*: corresponding to one who has merit) of the Lord unto all pleasing (in all areas of life), being fruitful in every good (*agathos*: benefit) work, and increasing (aorist passive) in the knowledge (*epignosis*: knowledge from the Holy Spirit) of God;

The production of fruit is good works in the Christian life. The word "may" in the *New King James* indicates potential; knowledge, walking in the Word, and victory are potential. People often know the Word but are not applying it in their lives. Faith without works is dead (James 2:17).

Just as the Colossian saints, we are to be growing in the knowledge of Him. Only by growth in the Word and walking in the Spirit can we produce divine good.

F. Divine Good

There are two sources of good:

1. Human good

   a) From the flesh of the believer

   b) From the flesh of the unbeliever

2. Divine good from the Spirit-controlled life of the believer

   a) Divine good from the flesh is impossible (1 Corinthians 13)

   b) Divine good means stability in life (2 Corinthians 9:8, 2 Thessalonians 2:17)

   c) Divine good is the basis for all rewards at the judgment seat of Christ (1 Corinthians 3:10–15, 2 Corinthians 5:10)

1:11 strengthened with all might, according to His glorious power, for all patience and longsuffering with joy;

Strengthened (*dunamoo*: by every enabling power), with all might (*dunamis*: miraculous power) according to (*kata*: the standard of) his glorious power (*kratos*: God's ruling power), unto (*eis*: resulting in) all patience (*upomeno*: endurance) and longsuffering (*makrothumia*: stability) with joyfulness;

God strengthens us for Christian life service with the same standard of the power of His glory. This is the power by which He rules the universe and the power by which He raised Jesus from the dead (Ephesians 1:19–21). This power is not just to get us "things" or cause us to enjoy the Christian life, but to bring us successfully through trials and tribulations. The trials we face are opportunities to apply the promises of God to our situation.

As we understand and walk in God's Word, we are empowered with God's strength. God's ultimate will is that we have patience to go through trials (which strengthens us)and become a witness and encouragement to others. Those who are carnal believers or unbelievers cannot experience God's joy in adverse circumstances.

G. The Inheritance of the Saints in Light

1:12 giving thanks to the Father who has qualified us to be partakers of the inheritance of the saints in the light.

Giving thanks (*eucharisteo*: constantly offering thanksgiving [1 Thessalonians 5:18]) unto the Father, which hath made us meet (*kausoo*: qualified) to be partakers of the inheritance of the saints in light.

As saints in light, we have an inheritance. What does the Scripture tell us about our inheritance?

1. Christ is the heir of all things (Hebrews 1:2).

2. Our inheritance is related to predestination (Ephesians 1:11).

3. Our inheritance is related to election (Hebrews 9:15). We share Christ's election.

4. Our inheritance is based on the death of another (Hebrews 9:16–17).

5. Our inheritance is based on sonship which we receive when we accept Christ as Savior (Romans 8:16–17).

6. Our inheritance is provided by grace (Titus 3:7).

7. Part of our inheritance is given now through the earnest of the Holy Spirit (Ephesians 1:13–14).

8. The greater portion of our inheritance is yet to come in eternity (1 Peter 1:4–5).

9. Salvation is the qualification for our inheritance (Colossians 1:12–13).

1:13 He has delivered us from the power of darkness and conveyed *us* into the kingdom of the Son of His love,

Who hath delivered us (*rhuomai*: once and for all rescued us) from (*ek*: out from) the power (*exousia*: authority) of darkness, and hath translated (transferred) us into the kingdom of his dear Son (the Son of His love):

Being bound in prison, Paul feels what all prisoners feel when looking through bars at the free world outside and so uses terms of deliverance from bondage into freedom. The new birth is far greater than any natural deliverance. God takes us from one kingdom (of darkness and death) into another kingdom (of eternal life and light) — the kingdom of the Son of His great affection.

H. The Ransom Has Been Paid

1:14 in whom we have redemption through His blood, the forgiveness of sins.

In whom (the Son of His love) we have (*echo*: own, possess) redemption (*apolutrosis*: the releasing effected by the payment of a ransom) through his blood, even the forgiveness (*aphesis*: cancellation, remission) of sins.

We were held hostage in Satan's kingdom, but Jesus came and redeemed us with a ransom price. Spiritual death entered from the outside in through Adam; redemption (spiritual life) entered from the inside out through Jesus. Jesus came to undo what Adam did. Adam and Eve voluntarily walked into the slave market. Children born to slaves are slaves. Jesus was the only man that could pay the redemption price because He was born into the earth without the nature of the flesh. He was tempted from the outside, just as Adam and Eve had been but did not sin. God paid the ransom price for the slavery of mankind, and the medium of exchange was the blood of the Lord Jesus Christ.

I. Redemption

1. The principle of redemption is found in John 8:31–36. We are born slaves and must be purchased by a free man (virgin birth qualified Jesus as our Redeemer).

2. Jesus paid the ransom for our sins on the cross (Psalm 34:22, Galatians 3:13, 1 Peter 1:18–19) with his blood (spiritual death).

3. Redemption is a doctrine believers can apply in times of pressure and receive blessing (Job 19:25–26).

4. Redemption results in the biblical doctrine of adoption (Galatians 4:4–6). We become adult sons.

5. Redemption was typified in the Old Testament by the shedding of blood (Hebrews 9:22).

6. Redemption provides the basis for the believer's inheritance (Hebrews 9:15).

7. Jesus's blood in redemption includes the forgiveness of sins (Colossians 1:14, Ephesians 1:7).

8. Redemption provides the basis for justification (Romans 3:24).

J. Results of Redemption

1. We are redeemed from the curse of the law (Galatians 3:13, 4:4–6).

2. We have sanctification (Ephesians 5:25–27).

3. We have been given authority over demonic powers (Colossians 2:14, 15; Hebrews 2:14–15).

4. We are guaranteed a resurrection body (Romans 8:23; Ephesians 1:14, 4:30).

K. The Blood of Jesus

1. Blood is the seat of animal life (Leviticus 17:10, 14).

2. Animal blood was used in Old Testament sacrifices to represent the spiritual death of Jesus on the cross (Leviticus 1–3, Colossians 1:20, Hebrews 10:19, 13:20; 1 Peter 1:2).

3. Redemption was portrayed in the Old Testament by means of animal blood (Hebrews 9:22).

4. Jesus did not die on the cross by bleeding to death (John 19:30, 33, 34), but of his own free will (Matthew 27:50, Luke 23:46, John 10:18).

5. The blood of Jesus represents His spiritual death when he bore our sins (2 Corinthians 5:21, 1 Peter 2:24).

6. The blood of Jesus represents four doctrines of salvation:

An act ✗a) Expiation (Revelation 1:5)

of making b) Redemption (Ephesians 1:7, Colossians 1:14, 1 Peter 1:18–19)

comments c) Justification (Ephesians 5:9)

        d) Sanctification (Hebrews 13:12)

7. The blood of Jesus also allows us to maintain fellowship with God (1 John 1:7, 9).

III. The Preeminence of Christ (15–22)

Verses 15 through 19 comprise the most concentrated section of scripture about the person of Christ. God always displays Himself through the second member of the Godhead (Jesus Christ). The Godhead is three unified as one. The Father plans, Jesus executes the plan, and the Holy Spirit reveals the plan.

1:15 ❡ He is the image of the invisible God, the firstborn over all creation.

Who is the image (*eikon*: impressed image, as a coin) of the invisible God, the firstborn (*prototokos*: firstborn, highest in rank) of every creature (*ktisis*: all creation):

A. Christ's Deity

1. Scripture reveals Christ as a member of the eternal trinity (Matthew 28:19, 2 Corinthians 13:14, 1 Peter 1:2).

2. There are outstanding scriptures dealing with the deity of Christ (Micah 5:2, John 1:1–3, 8:58; Romans 9:5, Titus 2:13, Hebrews 1:8–10, 1 John 5:20).

3. The preincarnate work of Christ shows His preexistence. He created the universe (John 1:3, Colossians 1:16, Hebrews 1:10).

4. The doctrine of divine decrees is found in Scripture (Psalms 2:7–9, 22:1–6, 40, 110). God declared His will in creation and redemption before the world began.

5. The only manifested member of the Godhead, Old Testament and New, is Christ. He often came as an angel (Jacob's wrestling match), or an object (Moses's burning bush). His main title was "the angel of the Lord." His title "Jehovah" is His redemptive and manifested title.

6. The characteristics of God are also ascribed to Christ:

    a) Eternal Life (Isaiah 9:6, Micah 5:2, John 1:1, 8:58; Ephesians 1:4, Colossians 1:16–17; Revelation 1:11)

    b) Righteousness and Justice (Luke 1:35, John 6:69, Hebrews 7:26)

    c) Love (John 13:1, 34; 1 John 3:16)

    d) Immutability (Hebrews 13:8) —unchanging in character [Covenant keeper]

    e) Omniscience (Matthew 9:4, John 2:25, 1 Corinthians 4:5) [knows everything]

    f) Omnipotence (Matthew 24:30, 28:13; 1 Corinthians 15:28, Philippians 3:21, Hebrews 1:3, Revelation 1:8) unlimited or great power

    g) Omnipresence (Matthew 28:20, Ephesians 1:23, Colossians 1:27) God is everywhere

B. Jesus Christ Was the Firstborn

1. The firstborn in Israel is given many privileges:

    a) Rulership

b) Priesthood

c) Heirship (which includes a double portion)

2. The Uniting of Humanity with Deity

As humanity, Jesus was the impressed image of God; as deity He was the exact or mirror image of God. Jesus performed miracles not because of His deity but because He was a human operating under the anointing of the Holy Spirit. God came into the earth in a tangible way through Jesus Christ.

C. The Hypostatic Union

Jesus Christ has two natures united without mixture or loss of either: human and divine, temporal and eternal (John 1:1–14, Romans 9:5, Philippians 2:5–11, 1 Timothy 3:16, Hebrews 2:14).

The incarnate person includes deity. Jesus is God, not a form of God. He is co-eternal with the Father and the Holy Spirit. The incarnation does not diminish His deity — He is an undiminished deity. He is not sub-God or inferior God, and Jesus did not lower Himself to become a man.

The incarnate person of Christ also includes true humanity — spirit, soul, and body — minus the old sin nature (the nature of the flesh). By means of the virgin birth, Jesus avoided the fallen nature of Adam. In His humanity He studied the Word and fellowshipped with the Father through the Holy Spirit (Luke 2:40, 52; John 1:14).

Jesus Christ is different from God in that He is man and yet different from man in that he is God. He is one hundred percent God and one hundred percent man. He is totally unique. No one has ever existed like Him before, and no one will ever exist like Him again. Jesus Christ as the God-man could be omnipotent and weak at the same time, omniscient and ignorant, awake yet asleep, self-existent yet hungry.

It was necessary for Christ to become humanity. Jesus Christ is the only means of salvation, satisfying both the claims of God and the claims of man. He served three primary roles:

1. Savior: As God, He could not die. Eternal life cannot die. Omnipotence cannot weaken itself and die. He had to become a man to die, and only his humanity died on the cross (Philippians 2:7–8, Hebrews 2:14–15).

2. Mediator: Someone who pulls two parties together and must be equal with both.

3. Priest: A man who represents man before God (Hebrews 7:4–5, 14, 28, 10:5, 14).

D. Son of David

God promised David he would have a son who would reign forever (2 Samuel 7:8–16, Psalm 89:20–37). A man was necessary to fulfill God's covenant with David. The incarnation was that fulfillment.

> **1:16 For by Him all things were created that are in heaven and that are on earth, visible and invisible, whether thrones or dominions or principalities or powers. All things were created through Him and for Him.**

For by (*oti*: because of, by means of) him were all things created (*ktizo*: formed, shaped, receive creation) (passive voice: receive creation) that are in heaven, and that are in earth, visible and invisible, whether they be thrones, or dominions, or principalities, or powers . . .

This verse tells of the creation of the universe, both spiritual and natural kingdoms, by the spoken word of the Lord (Genesis 1:3, Hebrews 1:3). It also lists all created things as visible (earth) or invisible (heaven). The first two (thrones and dominions) are visible and the last two (principalities and powers) are invisible.

E. Visible

1. Thrones (*thronos*): This is the governmental system we see in operation every day on the national, state, and local levels.

2. Dominions (*kuriotes*): These are the actual people who occupy the "thrones" and fulfill the positions as governors, mayors, etc.

F. Invisible

1. Principalities (*arche*): The demon rulers controlling the world systems (Ephesians 1:21, 2:2, 6:12).

2. Powers (*exousia*): These are the satanic beings, including the highest ranking member, Satan himself.

. . . all things were created by (*dia*: through) him and for him (for his use).

Hebrews chapter 1, verses 1 through 4 is a parallel passage to Colossians chapter 1, verses 16 and 17. This passage tells us that in His deity, the Lord created all things. Then, after His death, resurrection, and ascension, He was appointed heir of all things (even angels) and we have become joint-heirs of all things through the new birth and positional truth. We have an inheritance because we are in Him and share His heirship. We have destiny because we are in Him and share His destiny.

G. God's Will for Mankind in Eternity Past

1. Election

Election is the expression of the sovereignty of God before the human race, the universe, or anything else that existed except God. Election is also the expression of God's will for mankind long before anything else existed. God willed the very best for the human race in eternity past.

2. Grace Provision

Predestination is the provision of the sovereignty of God for mankind in eternity past to execute God's plan, purpose, and will. Predestination is the grace provision of God the Father for the royal family.

3. Eternity Past

Christ was predestined in eternity past (Isaiah 42:1, 1 Peter 2:5).

4. Destiny

The believer shares the destiny of Christ (Ephesians 1:4–5).

5. Hell

The unbeliever is not predestined to hell (John 3:18, 36).

6. Predestination

The Greek word for predestination is *proorize,* and it means to predesign. The following are examples of predestination:

  a) The crucifixion of Jesus (Acts 2:23)

  b) Victory for believers during suffering (Romans 8:28)

  c) Provision for the believer for time and eternity (Romans 3:28–29)

  d) Grace for propitiation (Romans 3:25) _appeasing God_

  e) The believer's life (Romans 9:11)

  f) The life and work of Jesus (Ephesians 1:9, 1 Peter 1:2, 20; 2 Timothy 1:9)

g) All assets for time and eternity (Ephesians 2:10)

H. The Sustaining Power of Christ

1: 17 And He is before all things, and in Him all things consist.

And he is (*eimi*: to be, to exist, to be present) before all things, and by him all things consist.

There was a time when "all things" began. Salvation was a fact before "things" were created. Science cannot tell us why "all things" hold together, but the Bible can:

1. Christ Is Sustainer of the Universe

a) Christ has always held the universe together. He created all things. In His deity, He was holding all things together even as a baby in the manger (Hebrews 10:5).

b) Christ holds the universe together for the sake of the Church, so that they can bring others into sonship (Hebrews 2:10). We are His prize and the apple of His eye and we are the reason He holds the universe together.

c) The universe was made and is sustained by the Word of God (Hebrews 1:3).

2. Scientific Law Does Not Exist

To have law, it must be enforced. Science cannot enforce the law. What sustains the universe is divine law, and Christ enforces that. Science observes these laws but cannot guarantee them. Christ, on the other hand, guarantees these laws because He sustains them.

3. Science Makes Assumptions

Science assumes that the laws of the universe will always be so, but the Word tells us they will one day change (2 Peter 3:10–12, Revelation 20:11).

4. Science Must Line Up with the Word

Many people today try to line up the Word with science. However, it is science that must line up with the Word or stand in error.

I. Christ the Head

1:18 And He is the head of the body, the church, who is the beginning, the firstborn from the dead, that in all things He may have the preeminence.

And he (Jesus) is (*eimi*: to be, to exist, to be present) the head (*kephale*: superior in rank) of the body (*soma*), the church (*ekklesia*); who is the beginning, the firstborn (*protokos*) from (*ek*: out from) the dead; that in all things he might have the preeminence (*proteuo*: highest rank).

The Greek word *kephale* for "head" is used in many New Testament passages and refers to the highest in rank (Romans 12:5, 1 Corinthians 11:3, 12:12–13). The "head" of the Church is in heaven; the "body" of the Church is on earth. Jesus did not become the "head" and the church did not become the "body" until after the resurrection. Located in the head is the brain that sends signals to the rest of the body. Our headship is in Christ, from which come our commands through the Word and by the Holy Spirit. This is why believers are said to have "the mind of Christ."

J. The Church

1. *Ekklesia*

Through positional sanctification — a result of our union with Christ — believers become part of the church. "Church" comes from the Greek word *ekklesia.* There are four other uses of the word *ekklesia* in the New Testament:

> a) An assembly of citizens to vote (Acts 19:25).
>
> b) An assembly of the Jews (Acts 7:38).
>
> c) An assembly in the synagogue (Matthew 18:17).
>
> d) A Local church (1 Corinthians 1:2, 1 Thessalonians 1:1).

2. Synonyms for Christ and the Church

> a) "Last Adam" and "the new creation."
>
> b) "Head" and "the body" (Ephesians 1:22–23, 4:4–5; Colossians 1:18).
>
> c) "Shepherd" and "sheep" (John 10, Hebrews 13:20, 1 Peter 5:4).
>
> d) "Vine" and "branches" (John 15).
>
> e) "Chief Cornerstone" and "lively stones" of the building.
>
> f) "High Priest" and "royal priesthood" (Hebrews 7:25, 10:10–14; 1 Peter 2:5, 9; Revelation 19:6–8).
>
> g) "Bridegroom" and "bride" (2 Corinthians 11:2, Ephesians 5:25–27, Revelation 19:6–8).

K. The Church Age

Dispensationally, the church age was a mystery (Romans 16:25–26, Ephesians 3:1–5) and thus unknown in the Old Testament.

1. It began on the Day of Pentecost (Acts 1).

2. It will be terminated at the rapture (1 Thessalonians 4:13–18).

3. Uniqueness of the church age:

    a) The new birth

    b) Universal indwelling of Christ

    c) Universal indwelling of the Holy Spirit

    d) Universal priesthood of believers

    e) Every believer represents Christ and is in full-time Christian service

    f) Intensification of demonic activity because of so many representatives of Christ

    g) A supernatural way of life, being led by the Holy Spirit

    h) The Word of God revealed to all believers

L. Reconciled Through the Blood of Jesus

1:19 ¶ For it pleased *the Father that* in Him all the fullness should dwell,

For (*oti*: because) it pleased (*eudokeo*: he has determined to approve, to think well of) the Father that in him should all fullness (*pleroma*: to fill a deficiency) dwell (permanently abide):

The fullness that dwelled in Christ was all things spiritual and natural. Because we are "in Him," we also share His fullness. All the fullness of God the Father includes everything that we have positionally in Christ.

1:20 and by Him to reconcile all things to Himself, by Him, whether things on earth or things in heaven, having made peace through the blood of His cross.

And, having made peace (*eirene*: make peace) through the blood of his cross (spiritual death), by him to reconcile (*apokatallaso*: restitution between two warring parties) all things unto (*eis*) himself; by him, I say, whether they be things in earth (man), or things in heaven (principalities).

Jesus made reconciliation on the cross and in Satan's domain — the earth and the atmosphere (Ephesians 2:1–2) — to forever settle the issue that Satan and his demonic powers have been subdued and the battle is over. We have been given authority over Satan and his demons because of reconciliation.

1. Reconciliation is the removal of the barriers between God and man (Ephesians 2:16, 2 Corinthians 5:18, Colossians 1:20–21). For every barrier, God has a solution:

    a) **Problem**: Sin

    Solution: Unlimited Atonement (2 Corinthians 5:14–15, 19; 1Timothy 2:6, 4:10; Titus 2:11, Hebrews 2:9, 2 Peter 2:1, 1 John 2:2)

    b) **Problem**: Penalty of Sin _____ atonment making amends

    Solution: Expiation (Colossians 2:14, Psalm 22:1–6)

    c) **Problem**: Physical Birth   renewal

    Solution: Regeneration (John 3: 1–18, Titus 3:5)

    d) **Problem**: Human Good   a charge or claim

    Solution: Imputation of God's Righteousness (Romans 3:22, 9:30, 10:10; 2 Corinthians 5:21; Philippians 3:9)

    e) **Problem**: Character of Man ___ To appease

    Solution: Propitiation (Romans 3:22–26, 1 John 2:1–2)

    f) **Problem**: Adamic Position   Pertaining to Adam

    Solution: Position in Christ (1 Corinthians 15:22, 2 Corinthians 5:17, Ephesians 1:3–6)

2. Because Jesus went to the cross and took upon himself every penalty of the barrier, the only remaining barrier is Christ Himself. The issue for salvation is now acceptance or rejection of Jesus.

3. The cross is the basis for reconciliation. The barrier is removed through Jesus's spiritual death.

4. In reconciliation, man is regarded as the enemy of God (Romans 5:10).

5. Believer's in the church age have the ministry of reconciliation (2 Corinthians 5:18–20).

6. Reconciliation creates peace between God and man (Ephesians 2:14, 16; Colossians 1:20).

7. Among the Levitical offerings, there are peace offerings. This portrays reconciliation (Leviticus 3, 8:15). God provided reconciliation.

1:21 ❡ And you, who once were alienated and enemies in your mind by wicked works, yet now He has reconciled

And you, that were sometime (at one time) alienated and enemies in your mind (*dianoia*: thoughts) by wicked (*paneros*: hurtful, evil, calamitous, derelict, vicious) works (*ergon*: human good), yet now hath he reconciled

Our separation from God was from the source of the carnal nature (flesh). It controlled our actions and thoughts. Our actions are sins and human good. Our thoughts were controlled by our mind, which was under the control of the nature of the flesh (Isaiah 55:6–9, Ephesians 2:3). Sin begins with thoughts. Uncontrolled thoughts eventually become actions. Thoughts and actions keep a person in captivity.

God is no longer at war with us. Instead He is at peace with us. This is reconciliation and the ministry of reconciliation that God has given to us (2 Corinthians 5:19–20). The good news is we are reconciled to God through the work of Jesus, not our own works. Even though we may still be lost in our trespasses and sins, God does not reconcile us because of us but because of His Son Jesus Christ.

1:22 in the body of His flesh through death, to present you holy, and blameless, and above reproach in His sight—

In the body of his flesh through death (*thanatos*: to be deadly), to present (*paristomi*: consecrate) you holy (*agio*) and unblameable (*amamos*: without blame) and unreproveable (*anegkletos*: irreproachable, unaccused) in his sight:

The new birth and its ultimate purpose in God's sight is our sanctification (Ephesians 5:27). The first thing available to us through the death of Jesus is our salvation. This is a gift. God loves to give gifts to men and watch them use those gifts to become like Him, walk just like Him, and bring Him glory.

The next thing available through his death is the potential of our sanctification and eternal rewards in heaven. This is a reward. Without the gift of eternal life, we could never have the indwelling Holy Spirit and ability to grow in the Word. Our spiritual growth allows us to live a lifestyle pleasing to God and overcome Satan's devices in the world. This builds up rewards in heaven (1 Corinthians 3:10–15). These rewards are all potential, based on obedience to the will of God.

IV. Paul's Admonition to the Saints at Colosse (23–29)

Paul admonishes the Colossian saints to continue in the Word that they have been faithfully taught by Epaphras.

A. Maturity Is a Result of the Word

1:23 if indeed you continue in the faith, grounded and steadfast, and are not moved away from the hope of the gospel which you heard, which was preached to every creature under heaven, of which I, Paul, became a minister.

If ye continue (*epimeno*: stay on top) in the faith grounded (on a firm foundation, founded) and settled (*agrolos*: stabilized), and be not moved away (swerving) from the hope (*elpis*: confidence, expectation) of the gospel, which ye have heard (*akouo*), and which was preached to every creature (all creation) which is under heaven; whereof I Paul am made (*ginomai*: became) a minister;

This verse begins an admonition that runs to the end of the chapter for the Colossian congregation to continue in the word they have been taught by Epaphras. Maturity comes from growing in the Word of God. The Word may be learned in the home or during study times. But nothing can replace the word presented by the minister to which you have submitted.

When you make up your mind to continue in the Word and not swerve from it, you become rooted, grounded, settled, and unmovable in the Christian life. You have hope in life that causes the world to take notice. Your life becomes a living witness before others and Satan cannot gain a hold on your life, family, business, or finances. You begin to lay up treasures in heaven and assure yourself of an abundant entrance into the everlasting kingdom (2 Peter 1:11).

1:24 ¶ I now rejoice in my sufferings for you, and fill up in my flesh what is lacking in the afflictions of Christ, for the sake of His body, which is the church,

Who now rejoice (*chairo*) in my sufferings for you, and fill up (*anapleroo*: fill a deficiency) that which is behind (lacking) of the afflictions (*thlipsis*: burden, tribulation, trouble) of Christ in my flesh for his body's sake, which is the church:

Verses 23 and 24 are both difficult passages to translate. Verse 23, though difficult on the surface, is not difficult at all when seen in the light of sanctification rather than salvation. Verse 24 stands correctly translated. Sufferings come to all believers, but these sufferings need to be defined. We will never suffer the agonies Jesus suffered for our sins and diseases. This occurred in the garden of Gethsemane and on the cross. This was spiritual suffering put upon Him by God the Father.

We will however, suffer the pressures and tribulations he suffered during his earthly ministry. The work of the cross is finished, but the sufferings that Jesus experienced in life are not over. The body of Christ faces these sufferings each and every day and will continue to be confronted with them until Jesus comes at the Rapture of the church.

Jesus told us we would suffer in life as He did (Matthew 5:10–12, John 15:20) and Paul told us the same (1 Thessalonians 3:4, 2 Timothy 3:12). In this passage, Paul gives us an example of how we are to handle suffering. We are to handle suffering with rejoicing. Part of perfection is not the suffering that we experience but how we come through that suffering. Suffering will come to us when we take on the needs of people and minister to others, but God has promised us victory in the midst of every trial and battle.

B. Paul's Responsibility and Burden

1:25 of which I became a minister according to the stewardship from God which was given to me for you, to fulfill the word of God,

Whereof (the church) I am made (*ginomai*: became) a minister, according to the dispensation of God which is given to me for you, to fulfill (*pleroma*: complete the deficiency of) the word of God:

There is a deficiency that all believers are to continue to fill, but there was one deficiency that Paul was given the responsibility to complete: The Word of God. The Word is complete — there is nothing to be added to it today (Revelation 22:19).

The completion of the Word of God was a great responsibility and a certain weight that hung around the apostles' necks at all times. Although the sufferings, trials, and afflictions that came from Satan weighed him down (2 Corinthians 11:21–33), Paul's burden from the Lord to complete the Word of God was far greater. He stood in a long line of prophets and apostles who wrote scripture. When Jesus rose from the dead and the Day of Pentecost began the Church Age, there was section of the Word of God left to be fulfilled: the New Testament epistles.

C. A Doctrine Unique to the Church Age: The Mystery

1:26 the mystery which has been hidden from ages and from generations, but now has been revealed to His saints.

Even the mystery (*musterion*: something hidden in the past but now revealed) which hath been hid (*apokrupto*: to keep secret) from ages (dispensations prior to the church age) and from generations (people who lived in those dispensations).

What had been kept secret in the heart of God and was lacking in the fulfillment of the Word of God was the "mystery." This was doctrine specifically for the church age. Acts 2 through Revelation 3 all involve the "mystery" of the church.

Musterion, translated as mystery, is a Greek word for the rights and teachings of ancient Greek fraternities known only to its members. Examples today would be groups like the Masons or the Scottish Rite. Jesus used this word with his disciples in Matthew 13:11 and Mark 4:10 and 11.

In the New Testament, the mystery refers to church-age doctrine (Ephesians 1:9, 3:2–10). This teaching begins with the day of Pentecost and continues until the rapture of the church. In the Old Testament, the period of time from the death to the ascension of Jesus was well documented because it occurred in the age of Israel. The tribulation, millennium, and eternal state are also well documented in the Old Testament because they are not part of the mystery and occur after the rapture of the church.

What else do we know about this mystery?

1. Its doctrine was not revealed in the Old Testament (Romans 16:25–26).

2. Part of it refers to the hardness of Israel during the church age (Romans 11:25).

3. The mystery was part of the divine decrees of eternity past, previously ordained by God (1 Corinthians 2:7, 4:1).

4. The rapture of the church is part of the mystery (1 Corinthians 15:51–53).

5. Some of the many new revelations and functions of the church age include:

    a) the individual priesthood of the believer.

    b) the indwelling of the Holy Spirit for every believer.

    c) the infilling of the Holy Spirit for every believer.

    d) the church.

    e) the body of Christ.

    f) the gifts of the Holy Spirit for every believer.

    g) apostles, prophets, evangelists, pastors, and teachers.

1:27 To them God willed to make known what are the riches of the glory of this mystery among the Gentiles: which is Christ in you, the hope of glory.

To whom (the saints) God would (*thelo*: inclined to, desire, be disposed) make known what is the riches of the glory of this mystery among the Gentiles; which is Christ in you, the hope (*ilpis*: confidence) of glory:

"Christ in you" refers to the indwelling person of Christ (the new birth) through the Holy Spirit in you. "Christ in you" also refers to the indwelling presence of Christ, who is the Word. The more Word we have in our lives, the more confidence we have toward the future. What brings confidence to our lives is not the new birth alone but the richness of the Word of

God dwelling in our hearts (Romans 8:28, 2 Corinthians 5:6, Philippians 4:11–13).

1:28 Him we preach, warning every man and teaching every man in all wisdom, that we may present every man perfect in Christ Jesus.

Whom (Christ) we preach (*kataggellion*: announce), warning every man, and teaching every man in all wisdom (*sophia*: wisdom from the word); that we may present every man perfect (*teleios*: mature) in Christ Jesus:

This should be the heart cry of every New Testament minister of the gospel: To preach to every person, then teach every person, and finally, present mature believers to God. We preach the gospel, first to the unbeliever, warning them of eternal destruction if they do not receive Jesus. When they do receive the Lord, we then teach them the Word of God so that they begin to grow in wisdom. We should strive for the perfecting of every saint so that they will live like God in Satan's world. The purpose of the new birth is so every man can be presented to the Lord in maturity (22–23).

Paul uses the term "we" in the presentation of the believer to the Lord at the judgment seat of Christ. Every minister has a part to play in the salvation and perfection of every saint.

1:29 To this *end* I also labor, striving according to His working which works in me mightily.

Whereunto (toward the perfecting of the saints) I also labour, striving (as an athlete striving to reach the finish line) according to his working (*energeia*: effectual working), which worketh (*energeia*) in me mightily (*dunamis*: miraculous power).

Paul has put all of his labor into the perfection of the lives of people. He is consumed with teaching the Word, which is the only thing that can bring maturity to the believer. All of the power in Paul's life comes from the internal power of his calling, the Word of God, and the anointing of the Holy Spirit.

Chapter Summary

Christ, the Head of the Church, is the visible image of the invisible God. All things are created by and for Christ, and it is because of Him that all things consist and are held together. Because of His death on the cross, we have been reconciled to God.

Although we will never suffer the agonies that Jesus suffered for our sin sand diseases, all believers will suffer the pressures and tribulations He suffered during His earthly ministry.

For church-age believers, the Word of God, especially the New Testament epistles, brings stability and confidence. It is the Word alone that will bring us success and fruitfulness in this life.

2:1–23 Living Free in Christ Alone

The Challenge of Chapter Two

No one is immune to false religion and legalism. That is why the most important thing in the Christian life is to become grounded and established in the Word of God (especially in the New Testament epistles). Man's religions, philosophies, and wisdom are vain and empty. It is in pursuing the Word of God as revealed by the Holy Spirit that we avoid the trap of religion and legalism that will put us into bondage. Positionally we are complete in Christ, but we must continually strive to grow in our understanding and knowledge of the Word, which is the Lord Jesus Christ.

I. The Colossian Problem: Gnosticism (1–8)

Paul wrestles in prayer for the believers at Colosse and Laodicea to increase in their understanding of the Word of God. Paul knows of the stability of faith that existed in the Colossian believers and also knows that the false teaching of Gnosticism has been introduced to destroy that stability.

A. Paul's Struggle

2:1 ¶ For I want you to know what a great conflict I have for you and those in Laodicea, and *for* as many as have not seen my face in the flesh,

For I would (*thelo*: wish, desire) that ye knew what (how) great conflict (*agon*: struggle in wrestling) I have for you (on your behalf), and for them at Laodicea, and for as many as have not seen my face in the flesh;

Paul begins by greeting the church at Colosse and letting them know of his spiritual struggle on their behalf. He also lets them know that he is experiencing the same struggle for the saints at Laodicea, which is the weakest of the churches in the Lycus Valley. Part of the challenge is new people added to both congregations who have never met Paul. Paul is addressing this admonition and prayer to all of the saints in both churches.

Paul's conflict is a wrestling match of prayer for the saints in Colosse and Laodicea because false religion was trying to enter the churches. True intercessory prayer is praying for an increase of the Word in the lives of believers. Paul prays for an increase of the Word for the believers who were in the churches that he had established (Ephesians 3:14–19). Paul's actions show that part of discipleship is not only seeing to it that a person comes to know the Lord, but that they also come to understand the Word and become grounded and settled in it (Isaiah 33:6).

2:2 that their hearts may be encouraged, being knit together in love, and *attaining* to all riches of the full assurance of understanding, to the knowledge of the mystery of God, both of the Father and of Christ,

That their hearts might be comforted (*parakaleo*: encouraged), being knit together (having been united) in love (*agape*: divine love from the Holy Spirit), and unto all riches (*plusios*: abundantly, richly) of the full assurance (*plerazo*) of understanding (*sunesis*: understanding, knowledge), to the acknowledgment (*epignosis*: revelation knowledge) of the mystery (*musterion*: New Testament epistles) of God, and of the Father, and (even) of Christ;

The content of Paul's prayer and his desire for every saint in Colosse is that their hearts would be knit together in love and that they would grow and have an understanding of the Word of God, especially the epistles. Hearts can only be comforted and congregations can only be knit together in love as they grow individually and corporately in the Word of God.

The same deficiency of the Word of God that existed in Paul's day exists in the church today. Every member of the body of Christ has a deficiency of the Word of God. Believers cannot become stable and established without the epistles. As each person fills the deficiency of the Word of God in his own life, stability will result.

We are not born again "smart"; we are born again "dumb," lacking in revelation knowledge of the Word. Paul tells us that part of his ministry was to see that all men understand his knowledge of the mystery of Christ which is the teaching of the epistles. The most valuable and precious writings of the Word of God are the new weapons of the New Testament epistles.

2:3 in whom are hidden all the treasures of wisdom and knowledge.

In whom (Christ) are hid all the treasures of wisdom (*sophia*) and knowledge (*gnosis*: natural knowledge).

The world is filled with knowledge (*gnosis*: natural knowledge). Amidst all of the knowledge that belongs to the world is a treasure (*epignosis*: revelation knowledge that comes from the Holy Spirit). The treasure that is hidden in all of the world's wisdom is found in Christ. To discover the "treasure" that is hidden in the world, we must first be "in Him."

To learn the entirety of the world's understanding is only to find *gnosis*. But only "the fear of the Lord is the beginning of knowledge" (Job 28:28, Psalm 111:10, Proverbs 1:7, 9:10). We will truly never begin our quest into revelation knowledge until we are born again and study the Word under the power of the indwelling Holy Spirit.

B. Power of the False Teaching of Religion

2:4 ¶ Now this I say lest anyone should deceive you with persuasive words.

And this I say (in Christ is found treasures), lest any man should beguile (*paralogizomai*: delude) you with enticing (*pithanologia*: persuasive) words.

This verse begins to tell us of the power a religious and intellectual group of people have to persuade Colossian believers to turn from the Word to philosophy. This group of people was mixing the philosophy of the times with the teachings of the Bible and deluding many Christians. People were being drawn away by a lower knowledge that was actually considered a higher knowledge.

2:5 For though I am absent in the flesh, yet I am with you in spirit, rejoicing to see your *good* order and the steadfastness of your faith in Christ.

For though (if) I be absent in the flesh, yet am I with you in the spirit, joying and beholding (*blepo*: seeing as with the eyes) your order, and the steadfastness (*taxis*: steadfastness in rank) of your faith in Christ.

Paul is in Rome at the moment and cannot see the believers in Colosse face-to-face or know of their order and steadfastness in faith. But, as their spiritual overseer, he sees clearly what is going on by the Spirit. He is filled with joy as he knows of their stability in the faith. He also knows that false teaching is being brought in to destroy this steadfastness and unity and scatter the believers.

2:6 ¶ As you therefore have received Christ Jesus the Lord, so walk in Him,

As ye have therefore received Christ Jesus the Lord, so walk (*peripateo*: forward movement a step at a time) ye in him:

We received Jesus Christ by faith in His Word, and we walk in Him through faith in His Word. Walking is always a picture of temporal truth or growth in God's kingdom.

C. Knowledge of God's Word Is the Key to Success

2:7 rooted and built up in Him and established in the faith, as you have been taught, abounding in it with thanksgiving.

Rooted and built up in him, and stablished (*bebioo*: stabilized) in faith, as ye have been taught, abounding (overflowing) therein with thanksgiving (*eucharisteo*: to be grateful, to give thanks).

We must be rooted before we can be built up. The Word establishes our foundation (roots), so we then may grow and withstand Satan's attacks (Ephesians 3:16–19, 4:14–15). Some believers always want "new" and "deep" things without any root, but that makes them gullible and easily taken in by false teaching.

"Rooted and built up" refers to reaching maturity (instead of living by feelings, emotions, and the senses, etc), wholly relying on the Word of God and the leading of the Holy Spirit. All of this knowledge of the Word comes through what we have "been taught." Paul here again, emphasizes the importance of a pastor for the spiritual growth of a Christian.

D. Paul's Warning

2:8 ¶ Beware lest anyone cheat you through philosophy and empty deceit, according to the tradition of men, according to the basic principles of the world, and not according to Christ.

Beware (*blepo*: see to it) lest any man spoil (*sulogogeo*: capture you, taken as a prisoner of war) you through philosophy (human reasoning) and vain (empty) deceit, after the tradition of men, after the rudiments (elementary teachings) of the world, and not after Christ.

> It is interesting to notice that Paul considers man's best attempt at education to be rudimentary (elementary or basic). This verse is telling us that even those who are built up in the Word are susceptible to being spoiled or taken captive by the philosophy and traditions of men. We never get to a place where we cannot be deceived.

Satan's main weapon is thoughts. The real key in life is our mind. If Satan has our thoughts, he has us. He comes to conquer our mind. Renewing the mind is a growing process. We can become either carnally minded or spiritually minded. Confusion, doubt, and unbelief all occur in the mind not in the spirit. This is why we are instructed to cast down imaginations and reasonings (1 Corinthians 10:3–5).

No Christain should ever think that he has arrived (1 Corinthians 10:12, Philippians 3:12–13) but should continue in the Word.

II. Victory through Christ (9–15)

Paul admonishes Colossian believers to realize that they are complete in Christ, and though they were at one time spiritually dead, they are now made alive through the death, burial, and resurrection of Jesus Christ. Paul also encourages the saints at Colosse concerning the fact that Jesus Christ spoiled principalities and powers — Satan and all of his demons — making an open show of their defeat and His complete triumph over them.

A. Undiminished Deity

2:9 For in Him dwells all the fullness of the Godhead bodily;

For (*oti*: because) in him dwelleth (*katoikeo*: is at home, permanently abides) all the fullness (*pleroma* [noun form]: to fill a deficiency) of the Godhead bodily.

"All the fullness" is a reference to the essence of God — His righteousness, love, eternal life, and everything else that characterizes Him. His diety was undiminished in the incarnation. When Jesus came into this earth as a baby and grew to a full-grown man, He was still as fully God as He had been before the foundation of the world, from eternity past. Jesus is one hundred percent God and one hundred percent man.

In verse 8, Paul tells us that man's wisdom, philosophy, and religion are empty and vain. When you study the person of Jesus Christ either from the standpoint of humanity or deity, endless dimensions of wisdom and knowledge will be found. You can never study Christ without finding fullness.

At one time there was a deficiency in the Word of God and Paul was to complete it (the epistles). Paul, in his day (and we in ours), are still completing the deficiency of the sufferings of the Lord Jesus Christ in our earthly walk.

There is a deficiency in our own lives of the knowledge of the mystery (written in the New Testament epistles), but there has never been, nor ever will be, a deficiency in the person of Christ. Our goal is to strive for the fullness of the Lord Jesus Himself. This gives us a lifetime to study and learn and never reach our goal. We will be learning forever, throughout all of eternity heading toward the goal of the fullness of Christ.

B. We Are Complete

2:10 and you are complete in Him, who is the head of all principality and power.

And ye are (*eimi*: be, you are and you do not get anymore that way) complete (*pleroo* [perfect middle participle]: to make full, complete) in him, which is the head of all principality and power (*exousia*: authority).

The word "complete" is in the perfect tense, which indicates something that was done in the past that has results right up until today. We may be growing in our knowledge and understanding of Him, but positionally, we are complete and will never grow any further. As complete (*pleroma*) as Christ is in deity (yet inside a human body), we are complete (*pleroma*) in our spirit, within our human body.

C. Positional Truth

Freedom demands security, and our security is knowledge of God's Word: "I will never leave you nor forsake you"; "No man can pluck them out of my hand"; "Stand fast therefore in the liberty wherewith Christ hath made us free"; "We have been made complete in Him."

1. Every believer receives positional truth at the moment of salvation (1 Corinthians 12:13, Acts 1:5, Ephesians 4:5, John 14:20).

2. Positional truth belongs to the carnal as well as to the spiritual believer (1 Corinthians 1:2, 30).

3. Positional truth protects the believer from judgment in eternity (Romans 8:1).

4. Positional truth qualifies believers to live with God for eternity which demands two qualities:

> a) God is perfect righteousness. Christ shares God's perfect righteousness and we have Jesus' righteousness (2 Corinthians 5:21).

> b) God is eternal life. Jesus has eternal life and we have eternal life when we receive Christ (1 John 5:11–12, 2 Corinthians 5:21).

5. Positional truth explains both election and predestination.

Election and predestination are two ways of describing the plan of God. Christ was elected to a destiny in eternity past. We share His election and destiny, hence we are predestined (Ephesians 1:3–6).

6. Positional truth produces a new creature in Christ (2 Corinthians 5:17).

7. Positional truth guarantees our eternity (Romans 8:38–39).

8. Positional truth exists in three categories:

> a) Retroactive positional truth: Deals with the past. Your past cannot be held against you (Romans 6, Colossians 2:12, 3:13; Ephesians 2:4–13).

> b) Current positional truth: We are now seated with Him in heavenly places (i.e. we rule over demons and principalities now).

> c) Future positional truth: We are guaranteed an eternity in heaven.

9. The implications of current positional truth:

> a) We share the righteousness of Christ (2 Corinthians 5:21).

> b) We share His life (1 John 5:11–12).

> c) We share His destiny (Ephesians 1:3–6).

> d) We share His election (Ephesians 1:4).

> e) We share His sonship (2 Timothy 2:1).

> f) We share His heirship (inheritance) (Romans 8:16–17).

g) We share His sanctification (2 Corinthians 1:2, 30).

h) We share His kingdom (2 Peter 1:11).

i) We share His priesthood (Hebrews 10:10–14, 1 Peter 2:9).

10. Characteristics of positional truth:

a) Positional truth is a gift of God, given through His sovereignty.

b) It is not progressive. It cannot be improved and is perfect at the moment it is received.

c) It is not related to human merit or good.

d) Positional truth is eternal in nature and cannot be changed by God, angels, Satan, demons, or man.

e) Positional truth is known only through the Word of God.

f) Positional truth is obtained in total at salvation.

D. Positional Sanctification

2:11 ¶ In Him you were also circumcised with the circumcision made without hands, by putting off the body of the sins[c] of the flesh, by the circumcision of Christ,

In whom (Christ) also ye are circumcised with the circumcision made without hands, in putting off (renunciation of) the body of the sins of the flesh by the circumcision of Christ:

This circumcision is a reference back to positional truth received at salvation, not to physical circumcision, sanctification, or spiritual growth. Every reference used for sanctification and growth has a corresponding analogy in positional truth.

The circumcision given to the men of Israel when they came into Canaan was a symbol of sanctification. Positional circumcision is all grace (without hands). Flesh is rejected (human help). We must realize this and continue to live by grace. Circumcision in this verse is a synonym for positional sanctification (1 Corinthians 1:30).

E. Circumcision

1. Circumcision means to cut around.

2. Circumcision was established as a sign of the Abrahamic covenant (Genesis 17:10–14) and had both physical and spiritual significance (Romans 4:9–11).

3. When Abraham was saved, he was a Gentile. There were no Jews. The Jews were a physical race that began with Abraham.

4. The ritual of physical circumcision has no spiritual significance in the church age (1 Corinthians 7:18–19, Galatians 5:2–3).

5. Titus, a church age minister, was not circumcised in order to make an issue of grace (Galatians 2:3). Titus was a Gentile who gave testimony to those who thought that circumcision was necessary for salvation.

6. Circumcision in the church age was a point of legalism (Acts 15:1, 24; Galatians 6:12–13).

7. Circumcision was used to show retroactive positional truth (Colossians 2:11).

8. No man is born circumcised. We are all born with the nature of the flesh and born-again (circumcised) afterwards. Circumcision was used to show the death of the flesh at salvation.

9. Physical circumcision is done after physical birth. Spiritual circumcision is done at the new birth to show the death of the flesh.

10. Old Testament circumcision was for males only. New Testament circumcision is for both men and women (Colossians 2:13).

F. The Baptism of Salvation

2:12 having been buried with *him* in baptism, in which you were also raised with him through your faith in the working of God, who raised him from the dead.

Buried with him in (by means of) baptism (aorist passive participle: having been buried with him), wherein also (in baptism) ye are risen with him through the faith of the operation (*energeia*: operational power) of God, who hath raised him from the dead.

This baptism is a reference to the new birth, the baptism of salvation (1 Corinthians 12:13). This is something for the church age only; it did not occur in any other dispensation. It was prophesied first by Jesus (John 14:20). It is the one baptism that makes us part of one body (Ephesians 4:5). It provides qualities not existent in physical birth (Galatians 3:26–28). It is the basis for positional truth (Romans 6:3–4, Ephesians 1:3–6, Colossians 2:10). It describes our union with Christ.

The word "baptism" means identification (i.e. a dye taking over a garment), dip, or immerse. Baptism is a symbol that a believer was spiritually dead but has been raised by Jesus Christ.

G. The Work of the Cross

2:13 When you were dead in your sins and in the uncircumcision of your flesh, God made you alive with Christ. He forgave us all our sins,

And you (plural: all believers), being dead (refers to spiritual death) in your sins and the uncircumcision of your flesh (old man), hath he quickened (given life) together with him, having forgiven (aorist middle of *charizomai*: graced) you all trespasses;

This begins a thought (13–15) that tells all Christ did for us in his death, burial, resurrection, and ascension into heaven. We were dead and could not do these things for ourselves.

The key word in this verse is "together" (cf. Ephesians 2:5, 6, 15). When we were spiritually dead, we believed on Jesus. This is the only thing we can do without doing anything. Faith is the total absence of human works. Our faith took us into retroactive positional truth called, in the previous verses, circumcision and baptism.

The first thing God did for us through Jesus was to make us alive. We could not give ourselves life because we were dead. We were held in bondage because of our personal sins and because of the nature of the flesh. For three days and three nights, Jesus laid beside us in death; this is identification. But when He was quickened, we were also quickened. God gave Jesus life first and through Jesus, we have life. Life came into us through the indwelling Holy Spirit.

The second thing God did for us through Jesus was to simultaneously forgive us our sins and trespasses.

2:14 having canceled the charge of our legal indebtedness, which stood against us and condemned us; he has taken it away, nailing it to the cross.

Blotting (canceling an IOU.; this is a gambler's term) out the handwriting or ordinances (*dogma*: absolute decrees) that was against us, which was contrary (hostile, at odds against) to us, and took it (*airo*: removed permanently) out of the way, nailing (having nailed) it to his cross;

The IOU we owed to God included perfect righteousness and holiness (everything Adam had in perfection). When Adam sinned, he put all of us in debt to God. What we owe is impossible to pay and doubly impossible since we were dead. Jesus canceled the IOU by nailing it to His cross (Ephesians 2:15). The third thing that God did for us through Jesus was to cancel the Law of Moses, which had kept us in captivity and away from salvation.

2:15 And having disarmed the powers and authorities, he made a public spectacle of them, triumphing over them by the cross.

And having spoiled (*apekdouomai*: disarm and throw away the weapons) principalities (*archon*: high ranking demons) and powers (*exousia*: officers), he made a show of them openly, triumphing (*thriambeuo*: leading a triumphal procession) over them in it (through him).

This verse goes back to the Roman custom of humiliating captured officers and high ranking officials by stripping them of their weapons and clothing and marching them through the streets naked. At the end of the march, many were publicly executed and the highest ranking officers and officials were executed first.

III. Religion: Satan's Counterfeit (16–23)

Paul warns the Colossian saints about the works required by Gnosticism and that the rules and regulations imposed by false religion are tools by which Satan could put them into bondage. He reminds them that because they have died with Christ, they have also been set free and the requirements of Gnosticism have no effect in overcoming the nature of the flesh.

A. Let No One Judge You

2:16 ¶ Therefore do not let anyone judge you by what you eat or drink, or with regard to a religious festival, a New Moon celebration or a Sabbath day.

Let no man therefore judge you (present active imperative of *krino*: stop letting anyone sit in judgment over you) in meat, or in drink, or in respect of an holy day.

1. The source of judgment is self-righteous, legalistic, carnal believers.

2. These people seek to build their righteousness on the five areas of Judaism mentioned in verse 16.

3. The weak or legalistic believer is the chief source of judgment on grace-oriented believers.

4. Those who do the judging are usually in the worst sins themselves. They meddle in the affairs of other believers, and they not only try to run lives but also try to fit others into their own mold.

5. Those judging are trying to pull splinters out of the eyes of others while they have logs in their own (Matthew 7:3–5).

6. You cannot build your righteousness on either someone else's un-righteousness or someone else's apparent failure to meet your standards.

B. Food and Eating

During the time of Israel, there were several food prohibitions which were taken by legalistic believers and distorted.

1. Pork was forbidden by the Mosaic Law.

2. Scavenger meat was forbidden by Mosaic Law.

3. Any food offered to idols was forbidden.

The object in the Christian life is spiritual food for the soul and not physical food for the stomach (Jeremiah 15:16, Matthew 4:4, Romans 14:2, 4, 17).

C. Drinking and Drunkenness

1. Drunkenness is a sin condemned in the Word (Proverbs 20:1, 23:20, Isaiah 5:11, 12, 28:7–8).

2. Drunkenness is especially to be avoided by certain people who have responsibility, such as leaders in government (Proverbs 31:4–5).

3. Certain individuals in the Bible are condemned because of drunkenness:

   a) Noah (Genesis 9:21)

   b) Lot (Genesis 19:32–36)

c) Nabal (1 Samuel 25:36–37)

d) Ephraim (Isaiah 28:1)

4. Small amounts of alcoholic beverages are condoned under certain circumstances in the Word (Proverbs 31:6–7, 1 Timothy 5:23).

5. Too much wine leads to national disaster (Joel 1:4–6, Isaiah 28).

6. Water to Wine

The miraculous wine discussed in John 2:1 through 11 was an alcoholic beverage. However, by turning the water into wine, Jesus is neither condoning nor condemning drinking. He is proving another point. The water being turned to wine is a type of the Word turning into joy in our lives (Psalm 104:15, Judges 9:13).

D. Holy Days

1. The feasts of Israel were designed to teach the Word to the people, mainly the two advents of Jesus Christ. Feasts were related to the agriculture of Israel:

   a) **Passover**: The feast was held during the time of the latter rains or the barley harvest. Jesus was crucified on Passover.

   b) **Unleavened Bread**: Passover began a seven-day period called Unleavened Bread. Women dusted the house spotlessly clean. Jesus was in the heart of the earth during this feast atoning and cleansing our sins.

   c) **Firstfruits**: The feast was held at the time of the latter rains or the barley harvest. Jesus rose from the dead on Firstfruits.

   d) **Pentecost**: The feast was held at the time when the early figs ripened. The outpouring of the Holy Spirit and the beginning of the Church occurred on Pentecost.

   e) **Atonements, Trumpets, and Tabernacles**: These feasts occurred during the early rains or the time of sowing. These all speak of Jesus' second advent, judgments, and millennial kingdom.

2. From June to October, there were no feasts. This represents a gap in time, which refers to the church age before the dispersion of Israel resumes.

3. Today no spiritual growth can be attached to keeping these days. They tell us, as it did the Jews, of different aspects of redemption and the work of Christ. These holy days are to be studied, not observed.

. . . or in the new moon . . .

4. The New Moon Festival (Numbers 10:10, 28:11, Isaiah 1:13, Ezekiel 46:1) was a monthly holiday held on the first day of each month. It was a day set aside to begin the month by observing Jehovah.

E. Sabbath

. . . or of the sabbath day.

Saturday, the seventh day of the week, was set aside as a memorial to the grace of God. On this day the Jews rested and did not work in observance of God resting after the six days of creation. The Sabbath belongs to the Jewish Age, not the Church Age. Romans 14:4–10 tells us that we are to regard each day the same. The reason we consider Sunday as the day for assembled worship is because it is the day Jesus arose from the dead and also the day of Pentecost. Both of these days mark the beginning of our dispensation, therefore we traditionally observe Sunday as the day we worship together (1 Corinthians 16:1–2). Sabbath was designed by God to teach the principle of His grace (Genesis 2:2–3, Isaiah 58:11–14). *Sabbath* means, "to rest." God rested, not because He was tired, but because there was nothing left to do. His work was completed.

There is a temporal Sabbath and an eternal Sabbath. The temporal Sabbath is faith — resting on His promises (Hebrews 3:11). This can also be referred to as the "moment-by-moment" Sabbath (Hebrews 4:1–3). Eternal Sabbath is the imparting of eternal life at the moment of salvation (Matthew 11:28, John 20:31).

1. Weekly Sabbath

Sabbath was instituted as law; it was mandatory as a memorial to grace (Exodus 20:8–11, Leviticus 23:3).

2. Sabbatical Year

Every seventh year was a sabbatical year for Israel, which was also a memorial to grace (Exodus 23:10–11, Leviticus 25:3, 4, 26:33–36). Jewish failure to observe this was an indication of a failure to recognize God's grace.

3. Jubilee

The year of Jubilee occurred every fiftieth year, after seven sabbatical years (Leviticus 25:8). This was the great year of grace when all was restored, reminding each individual that it was the Lord who brought them to the place they were.

4. Profaning the Sabbath was associated with idolatry and apostasy (Ezekiel 23:37–39).

5. The scripture on Sabbath violation is found in Nehemiah 13:15–21.

6. Sabbath was set aside in the church age. This is taught in the book of Galatians and in Colossians 2:16–17.

7. The principle of worshiping on the first day of the week is found in Acts 20:7 and 1 Corinthians 16:2.

F. Shadows

2:17 These are a shadow of the things that were to come; the reality, however, is found in Christ.

Which are a shadow (*skia*: image cast by an object) of things to come; but the body (*soma*) is of Christ.

This is a reference to the previous verse, speaking of the Old Testament laws, which the Colossians were hearing and beginning to obey. Shadows are without substance but need substance in order to be formed (Hebrews 8:5, 10:1). There are no shadows in the Church Age. Christ is the reality of all shadows. Here is a summary of Verses 16 and 17:

1. The feasts, new moon festivals, and Sabbaths were shadows pointing to the reality: the coming life, death, and resurrection of Jesus Christ.

2. Shadows were a legitimate means of presenting the Word of God before Jesus came.

3. Jesus is the anticipated substance of the holy days and laws.

4. Once Jesus came, the shadows were replaced with substance — a physical body.

5. Substance also refers to the doctrine of the New Testament epistles (also known as the mystery).

6. To continue with shadows is an empty expression of legalism.

7. Shadows look forward to the cross, and the epistles look back.

G. Neither Visions nor Angels Form Doctrine

2:18 Do not let anyone who delights in *false* humility and the worship of angels disqualify you. Such a person also goes into great detail about what they have seen; they are puffed up with idle notions by their unspiritual mind.

Let no man beguile you (*katabrabeueto*: defraud you, declare you ineligible) of your reward in a voluntary humility (forced self-effacement) and worshipping of angels, intruding into (*embateuo*: scrutinizing minutely) those things which he hath ("not" is not found in the Greek) seen (Paul is taking his stand on visions), vainly (emptily) puffed up (inflated by pride) by his fleshly mind (sensual imagination).

Many of those who are spreading false doctrine in Colosse had actually seen a vision, been spoken to by an angel, or had seen into the realm of evil spirits. And seeing visions, being ministered to by an angel, and seeing into the realm of evil spirits are all part of the church age (Acts 2:17, 9:10–12, 10:1–3, 9–11). The problem is that doctrine contrary to the Word is being formed according to these experiences.

Any vision that does not line up with the Word of God is to be thrown out. The Word is always the final authority (2 Peter 1:19). Even if an angel were to appear and reveal something contrary to the Word, the angel is to be cursed (Galatians 1:8). Visions and words from angels do not form doctrine. Doctrine comes from the Word of God. The Word of God must be used to confirm the appearance of angels, visions, or any manifestation of the Holy Spirit.

Often an individual who has had a vision will scrutinize the vision over and over again, instead of scrutinizing the Word. And after dissecting the vision many times, the vision ends up being bigger than it was in the beginning. The imagination paints a picture greater than God had originally intended. Many books and ministries today are founded on visions or encounters with angels or demons. Instead of building up believers in the Word, they confuse the issue with personal stories or testimonies. Because the Word is replaced by manifestations, confusion results as many Christians try to build their lives on someone else's experience.

H. Nourished by the Word, United by the Spirit

2:19 and not holding fast to the Head, from whom all the body, nourished and knit together by joints and ligaments, grows with the increase *that is* from God.

And not holding (*karteo*: being occupied with) the Head (*kaphale*: one superior in rank), from (*ek*: from, out from, by) which (whom) all the body by joints and bands (*sundesmos*: ligaments) having nourishment ministered, and knit together, increaseth with the increase of God.

Verse 19 is talking about the Word. God has exalted His Word above His name. He has not exalted angels or visions above His name.

We first need nourishment and then to be knit together. What nourishes us is the Word of God, and what knits us together is the Holy Spirit (Ephesians 4:3). Both the Word and the Holy Spirit come to us from the Head, the Lord Jesus Christ. Jesus is the Word (John 1:3), and He sent us the Holy Spirit for power and unity (Acts 2:2, 33). This can only come as we are occupied with Jesus.

The problem with the Gnostics was that they were spending too much time looking into their visions and visitations. Instead of scrutinizing visions and visitations, we should be looking intently into understanding the Head, Jesus. This comes through more knowledge of His Word. We can only increase in two ways, the Word and the presence and power of the Holy Spirit. Both of these increases come from God Himself.

I. Paul's Response to the Influence of Asceticism

2:20 ¶ Therefore, if you died with Christ from the basic principles of the world, why, as *though* living in the world, do you subject yourselves to regulations—

Wherefore if (since) ye be dead (aorist active voice: you died) with Christ from the rudiments (*otoikeion*: elements) of the world (*kosmos*: the world), why as though (if) living in the world, are ye subject to ordinances (do you subject yourselves to decrees),

Doctrines built upon angels and visions result in legalism. Legalism requires people to live by rules and regulations. Since there is not word or grace attached, there must be systems of merit to attain the goals set by such teaching. The systems of spirituality are the same as goals set by the world for salvation. This all comes from religion. It is bad enough to be an unbeliever and be religious. It is worse to be a believer who becomes religious. Paul brings out areas of asceticism that were being taught for spirituality.

2:21 "Do not touch, do not taste, do not handle,"

Touch not; taste not; handle not;

"Touch not" is abstinence from sex. In Colosse, refraining from sex for long periods of time is being taught as a new level of spirituality. People begin to look at sex as unholy and abstaining from sex as a way to get closer to God.

"Taste not" is abstinence from certain kinds of food. Spirituality does not come through the types of food we eat or do not eat (Romans 14:17). Paul warns us that in the last days, (the days in which we are living), many Christians will turn from the faith to forms of religious abstinence (1 Timothy 4:1–5). Included in this admonition is refraining from sex and certain forms of food.

"Handle not" is refraining from violence. This is a distortion of the Word, promoting a passive lifestyle and living "at peace" according to the world's standard of peace rather than God's standard. This takes peace far beyond what God Himself intended. It is peace at all costs. This teaching advocates that to stay close to God, one must stay away from all forms of retaliation.

Abstinence in these areas is fine, but only if they are chosen as a personal lifestyle. God does not care how much sex goes on between a husband and a wife. If the husband and wife choose to refrain from sex for a time, in order to give themselves to prayer, this is acceptable with God. But refraining from sex does not make a person more spiritual, prayer does. The same is true with food. Fasting does not make a person more spiritual; the prayer and worship that take the place of eating do. Religion always puts more emphasis on the outward actions than on the pureness of the heart and attitude.

2:22 which all concern things which perish with the using— according to the commandments and doctrines of men?

Which all are to perish with the using; after the commandments and doctrines of men?

This is a poor translation. The Greek of the first part of this scripture reads "which things all lead to corruption." The things you believe will bring you closer to God actually lead you farther away from spirituality. Trying under your own strength to get closer to God causes you to end up farther away from Him. This is the ultimate destination of legalism; it leads you into more bondage and not liberty. It is a vicious cycle that can only be broken by the understanding of the Word and grace.

> **2:23 These things indeed have an appearance of wisdom in self-imposed religion, *false* humility, and neglect of the body, *but are* of no value against the indulgence of the flesh.**

Which things have indeed a show (*logos*: outward appearance) of wisdom in will (*ethelothreskeia*: voluntary) — worship and humility, and neglecting of the body; not in any honour to the satisfying of the flesh.

The Greek word *ethelothreskeia* is used to describe the misguided zeal of the religious. This zeal is mistaken for spiritual fervor and begins to infect the church at Colosse. It is a zeal more interested in the outward show of worship and asceticism than in a truly godly life. This appears as an outward display of wisdom, but the true wisdom that comes from God is missing. There is no Word backing their religious actions; they only have the appearance of worship, humility, and temperance. Instead of truly controlling the flesh from the spirit, the flesh is still as much in control as if they were sinning. Asceticism comes just as much from the flesh as lasciviousness. ✓

Chapter Summary

It is in Christ that all of the treasures of wisdom and knowledge can be found. Our goal is to become established in the truth of God's Word and united by the love of God. If our focus is on growing in the knowledge of the Word, we will avoid being drawn away by the philosophies and false religions of man.

Gnosticism was not only a threat to the Colossian church; it remains a threat to the church today under the guise of the New Age movement and other false religions. Performing certain acts, observing special days

Prosperity Movement

deemed holy, or abstinence as an avenue to holiness are all vanity in the eyes of God. Our pursuit should be to understand all that we are positionally in Christ so that we can walk in the freedom that He provided in His death, resurrection, and ascension.

3:1–25 Daily Demonstration of the Christian Life

The Challenge of Chapter Three

We are exhorted to keep our minds on things that are above. We do this by meditating daily in the Word. It is by keeping our minds fixed on the Lord that we have the power to overcome the works of the flesh. Through the power of the Word, we put off the old man and his evil deeds and put on the new man. As we look into the mirror of God's Word, the Spirit of God will change us into the very image of Jesus Christ.

When God's Word overflows in our hearts, it will be manifested through our lives in praise and worship to God and in admonition and instruction to others. Through the Word of God dwelling in us richly, we can become the best husbands, wives, children, employers, and employees as a witness to the world.

I. Challenge of Living the Christian Life (1–4)

Our life is hid with Christ in God and we are to set our affections on things above (our position in Christ), not on things of this earth. As we focus on who God sees us to be, we will begin to look and act more like Christ in this world.

A. Seek Those Things Which are Above

3:1 ¶ If then you were raised with Christ, seek those things which are above, where Christ is, sitting at the right hand of God.

If (since) ye then be risen (aorist passive: were raised) with Christ, . . .

Colossians 3 is the transitional chapter in the book of Colossians, taking us from the positional truths presented in chapters 1 and 2 to temporal truths, which begin in chapter 3.

The word "if" is in the first class condition meaning "since."

B. Four Class Conditions of "If"

1. **First Class Condition**: If means "if, and it is true"; "If thou be the Son of God . . . "(Matthew 4:3).

2. **Second Class Condition**: If means "if, and it is not true"; "If thou wilt worship me (Satan), all shall be thine" (Luke 4:7).

3. **Third Class Condition**: If means "if, and maybe it is true and if maybe it is not true."

4. **Fourth Class Condition**: If means "if, and I wish it were true, but I know it won't happen"; "But if ye suffer for righteousness' sake . . . " (1 Peter 3:14).

. . . seek (*zeteo*: pursue) those things which are above, where Christ sitteth (is sitting) on the right hand (side) of God.

"Things which are above" refers to positional truth. Our minds should daily be focused on who we are in Christ. By mediating on who we are in Him, we will strategically have victory over Satan. Our main battle and victory is in our thought life. "Seeking those things which are above" is having a mind that is stayed on the Lord. Following the new birth, the "renewed mind" is the main objective in the Christian life. Since the spirit man — the true and real man — is already seated in heaven with Jesus, our thoughts and attention should be there with Him also.

Jesus is seated in a place of power and authority; therefore, we are also because "as He is, so are we." If we see ourselves as above, we can only see Satan and his kingdom as beneath us.

There is a contrast between Colossians 3:1 and Colossians 2:20. Colossians 2:20 tells us "If you are dead with Christ from the base things of this world, live like a dead man." Colossians 3:1 says, "If you are risen with Jesus, live like those who are alive."

Colossians 3:1 tells us what to do but not how to do it; that is found in verse 2.

3:2 Set your mind on things above, not on things on the earth.

Set your affections (*phroneo*: mind) on things above, not things on the earth.

The key that is found in this verse is our thought life. This verse is a command.

C. Mental Attitude

As Christians, we have access to antithetical mental attitudes: our human viewpoint and reasoning and God's divine viewpoint and reasoning (Isaiah 55:7–9). Where we set our minds makes all the difference. What we think is really who we are (Proverbs 23:7).

Having a divine viewpoint is commanded for every believer (2 Corinthians 10:4–5), and since the Word is the mind of Christ, such intake shapes our mental attitude (1 Corinthians 2:16, Philippians 2:5). God's plan of grace demands a new mental attitude on the part of the believer (2 Timothy 1:7).

1. Inner happiness from the Word produces a capacity for the proper mental attitude — divine viewpoint (Philippians 2:2)

2. Mental attitude is attained from the infiltration of the Word (2 Corinthians 5:1, compare with verses 6 and 8).

3. Stability is a proper mental attitude (Philippians 4:7).

4. Giving begins as a mental attitude (2 Corinthians 9:7).

5. Love is a mental attitude (1 Corinthians 13:5).

6. Worldliness or evil is a mental attitude (Matthew 9:4, Romans 12:2, Galatians 6:3, and Colossians 3:2).

7. Sins of the thoughts (mental attitude) are the worst kind. Actions of sin (overt activities) are only a result of sins of thoughts (Proverbs 15:13).

D. Your Life is Hidden

3:3 For you died, and your life is hidden with Christ in God.

For ye are dead (aorist tense: you died), and your life (*zoe*: life) is hid (perfect middle: has been hid) with (together with) Christ in God.

Verses 1 and 3 set up another contrast. Verse 1 says you are alive and verse 3 says you are dead (cf. 2:20). Verse 3 combines both thoughts by saying you are dead and your life is hidden. This brings up the old and new man: the flesh and the spirit. While part of you is dead (the outward man), the other part is alive (the inward man) forever. We are to keep our attention on the part that is alive and not on the part which is dead.

E. When Christ Shall Appear

3:4 When Christ *who is* our life appears, then you also will appear with Him in glory.

When Christ, who is our life, shall appear (*thaneroo*: aorist passive: have appeared), then shall ye also appear (*thaneroo*: future passive subjunctive: to be made manifest) with him in glory.

This is a reference to the Rapture of the church, and our changing into the bride of Christ. This will occur when we receive our resurrection body (John 14:1–3, 1 Corinthians 15:51–55, 1 Thessalonians 4:13–17).

F. Manifestation of the Bride of Christ

The body of Christ is being formed on the earth during the church age (Ephesians 1:22–23, 2:16, 4:4–5, 5:23; Colossians 1:18, 24, 2:19). The church will reach full maturity at the judgment seat of Christ. When the body of Christ is complete, the rapture will occur (1 Thessalonians 4:16–18, 1 Corinthians 15:51–57).

1. But before then, during the tribulation, the bride of Christ is being prepared in heaven:

    a) By entering ultimate sanctification (1 Corinthians 15:51–57, Philippians 3:21, 1 John 3:1–2).

    b) By being cleansed from all human good (1 Corinthians 3:12–15).

    c) By being freed from the nature of the flesh.

2. The bride returns with Christ at the second coming (1 Thessalonians 3:13). At the return of the bride and groom, "Operation Footstool" occurs (Psalm 110:1). Three events will occur at this time:

    a) All unbelievers will be removed from the earth and put into hell.

    b) Satan will be imprisoned for one thousand years in the bottomless pit.

    c) All demons will also be removed and put into the bottomless pit with Satan (Zechariah 13:2, 1 Corinthians 15:24–25).

3. There will be a coronation of the groom as King of Kings (Revelation 19:6), and the wedding supper of the Lamb will occur (Revelation 19:7–9):

   a) The marriage will occur in heaven, but the supper will occur on earth (Matthew 25:1–13).

   b) The marriage supper is described in detail in Revelation 19:6–9.

   c) Four categories of people will be attending the marriage supper of the Lamb:

      1) The Bride: the church

      2) Friends of the Groom: Old Testament saints

      3) Friends of the Bride: Tribulational believers alive at the second coming

God is going to take us by force into the clouds (His glory) at the rapture of the church, and we will then become the bride of Christ.

II. Objective of Living the Christian Life (5–17)

God has given us the power and ability to "put off" the works of the flesh by "putting on" the new man. By renewing our minds with the knowledge of the Word of God, we are empowered to control our thoughts. This will cause us to be a witness in our actions before others.

A. Mortify the Deeds of the Flesh

3:5 ¶ Therefore put to death your members which are on the earth: fornication, uncleanness, passion, evil desire, and covetousness, which is idolatry.

Mortify (*nekroo*: render sexually dead, impotent) therefore your members (*melos*: body parts, all facets of the fleshly nature) which are upon the earth (*ge*: the entire earth); fornication (*phorneia*), uncleanness (*akatharsia*), inordinate affection (*pathos*), evil concupiscence (*epithumia*: desire, craving, longing, lust, desire for what is forbidden), and covetousness (*pleonexzia*), which is idolatry:

This verse is a command. Only when we keep our attention on the Lord and the position we have in Him do we have the power and ability to cast off the works of the flesh.

Several works of the flesh are brought out in this verse:

1. Fornication: illicit sex outside marriage, between a man and a woman.

2. Uncleanness: unnatural sexual vices such as homosexuality, lesbianism, bestiality, and pornography (Romans 1:24).

3. Inordinate Affection: passion which is depraved, abnormal sexual lusts leading to abnormal and excessive sexual acts like nymphomania: passions that control.

4. Evil Concupiscence: evil lusts for sex or anything else (i.e. lust for power or things).

5. Covetousness: insatiability, unfulfilled passions.

The essence of the Christian life is in the soul — in the thought realm. We offer our body as a living sacrifice by the renewing of the mind. The Spirit-controlled person has a body that is alive to the will of God. God sees no future for our fleshly body.

3:6 Because of these things the wrath of God is coming upon the sons of disobedience,

For which things' sake (because of which) the wrath of God cometh on the children of disobedience.

In the life of an unbeliever, the wrath of God comes because of the rejection of Jesus Christ as Savior. God's anger will also be displayed through divine discipline toward a believer who acts from his flesh.

3:7 in which you yourselves once walked when you lived in them.

In the which (i.e. the sins of v. 5) ye also walked (*peripateo*) some (at one) time, when ye lived (*zao*) in them.

Paul is telling the Colossians that when a believer walks after the flesh, they are walking like an unbeliever. Carnal Christians are said to be "sleeping among the dead"; it is difficult to distinguish between a sleeping person and a dead person. The carnal Christian looks and acts just like an unbeliever (1 Corinthians 3:3, Ephesians 5:14).

B. The Command to Put Off

3:8 ¶ But now you yourselves are to put off all these: anger, wrath, malice, blasphemy, filthy language out of your mouth.

But now (change of attitude) ye also put off (*apotithomi*: put aside or away) all these (*tapanta*: all, everything); anger (*orge*: indignation), wrath (*thumas*: explosions of anger, violent outbursts), malice (*kakia*: vengeance, the desire to defame or injure others), blasphemy (*blashpemia*: to malign or slander others), filthy communication (*aischrologia*: filthy language, obscenity) out of your mouth.

There is a tendency to think if we are not committing outward sexual sins (controlled by the sin of lust), that we are right in our walk with God. Paul now tells the Colossians that there are other sins that can be committed by Christians; these are sins of the thoughts and the tongue. People often excuse these sins as personality quirks or the way they were born, but these sins can be "put off" like old clothing through the power of the new birth, the strength of the Word, and the Holy Spirit.

Taking off clothing and putting on new clothing does not require much strength. In the same way, putting off the sins mentioned in this verse requires little strength or effort. We are to use the strength that we have been given through the Word of God and by the Spirit of God to "put off" sin in our lives.

3:9 Do not lie to one another, since you have put off the old man with his deeds,

Lie not one (*pseudo*: do not speak falsely) to another, seeing that ye have put off (*apekduomai*: stripped off, spoiled, disarmed) the old man with his deeds (methods of operation);

In verse 8, "putting off" is the Greek word *apotithomi*. This putting off is in reference to the deeds or the manifestations of the flesh. In verse 9, "putting off" is the Greek word *apekduomai*, a violent word for disarming an enemy or causing spoil. This is not only conquering enemies, but further humiliating them by stripping off their medals and making a public display of them.

In verse 9, we have the culprit, the one causing the deeds, which is the nature of the flesh.

The same Greek word used for "spoiled" in Colossians 2:15 (*apekdouomai*) — which described what Jesus did to Satan and the demons at His resurrection — is also being used in this verse. Through the new birth and by the power of the Word, we have been given the ability to put off, like clothing, the deeds of the flesh. And just as Jesus stripped and humiliated the powers of hell at the resurrection, we can strip and humiliate the nature of the flesh.

C. The Command to Put On

3:10 and have put on the new *man* who is renewed in knowledge according to the image of Him who created him,

And having put on (*enduo*: dressed yourself in) the new man which is renewed (*anakainoo*: being renewed) in knowledge (*epignosis*: revelation knowledge from the Holy Spirit; this is not a natural knowledge) after (*kata*: according to) the image (*eikon*: exact image) of him (Jesus Christ) that created him (the new man):

Up until now, we have only been told what to do. We are to put off the old man, stop lying, and stop acting on the deeds of the flesh. Now in verse 10, we are told how to accomplish that: by putting on the new man — the spirit man — which can now control our thinking and actions. The new man is the recreated spirit in the believer. Once he controls the thinking, the result is true spirituality (Romans 8:6).

Putting off the old man and his deeds and putting on the new man is something every Christian does. God has done many things for us, but he also gives us the ability to do things for ourselves. This verse tells us that as we grow in knowledge, our inward man is reshaped by revelation knowledge into the same image as Jesus Christ.

The word *eikon* implies an exact image as in sculpting or carving. The Greek word *charachter* is different in its meaning. It denotes an impressed or stamped image (translated "express image" in Hebrews 1:3). Jesus was the impressed image of God in the earth and the inward man is being formed daily into the exact image of Jesus Christ. The Word of God is the mirror, and the Spirit of God sculpts the inner man until he looks like Jesus Christ.

3:11 where there is neither Greek nor Jew, circumcised nor uncircumcised, barbarian, Scythian, slave *nor* free, but Christ *is* all and in all.

Where (in which place? In the new man) there is neither (does not exist) Greek nor Jew (cultural), circumcision nor uncircumcision (racial), Barbarian, Scythian (political), bond nor free (social): but Christ is all, and in all.

This scripture is a reference to positional truth. The object of the Christian life is our outward life — our temporal existence — growing up to match our position or union with Christ.

Sanctification is the object of the previous verses, and verse 11 now becomes the goal: to be conformed to the image of Christ.

There are no racial, social, or sexual distinctions in our union with Christ (our position in Him as the body of Christ). Because Jesus Christ lives in each one of us through the Holy Spirit, we need to see Him in others rather than their color, social status, or nationality. In our daily living, this should be our attitude. Positional truth should guide temporal truth.

3:12 ¶ Therefore, as *the* elect of God, holy and beloved, put on tender mercies, kindness, humility, meekness, longsuffering;

Put on (*enduo*: dress yourself, put on, clothe one's self) therefore, as the elect (elected ones) of God, holy (*agios*: most holy thing) and beloved (*agapao*: to love dearly), bowels (*splagchnon*: seat of tender affections — kindness, compassion, etc.), of mercies (*oiktrimos*: compassion), kindness (*chrestotes*: disposition of grace toward others), humbleness of mind (*tapeiphrosune*: disposition of grace toward yourself), meekness (*prautes*: remaining teachable), longsuffering (*makrothumia*: the expression of patience and steadfastness in your faith toward others);

This verse is telling us to look at others and ourselves as God looks at us. Since He sees us as elect and this becomes the basis of His love and patience toward us, it should also be the basis of our love and patience toward others.

D. Election

1. All members of the human race are potentially elected to the plan of God through unlimited atonement (2 Timothy 2:10).

2. Christ was elected from eternity past (Isaiah 42:1, 1 Peter 2:4, 6)

3. Election of Christ was decreed before the foundation of the world (John 15: 16, Ephesians 1:4, 2 Thessalonians 2:13, 1 Peter 1:2).

4. Election for the believer means sharing the election of Christ as well as His destiny. Every believer shares the election of Christ through positional truth (Romans 8:28–37, 1 Corinthians 1:24–30, Ephesians 1:4).

5. Election is the present as well as the future possession of every believer (John 15:16, Colossians 3:12).

6. This election is ours from the moment we believe in Christ (1 Thessalonians 1:4, 2 Thessalonians 2:13, 2 Timothy 1:9).

7. Election is the foundation of the church (1 Thessalonians 1:4).

8. Orientation to election comes from understanding the Word and positional truth (Titus 1:1).

3:13 bearing with one another, and forgiving one another, if anyone has a complaint against another; even as Christ forgave you, so you also *must do.*

Forbearing (*anecho*: endure, stand your ground in love with) one another, and forgiving (*charisomai*: forgiving in grace, no strings attached) one another, if any man have a quarrel (complaint) against any: even as Christ forgave you, so also do ye.

This is a warning, even to those who are approaching the high spiritual plane of happiness and prosperity. It is possible to falter at any level of spiritual growth through unforgiveness.

The Bible has many warnings against being out of fellowship and being hindered in spiritual advancement (Psalm 66:18, Matthew 7:1–5, 22, 25, 18:21–35).

3:14 But above all these things put on love, which is the bond of perfection.

And above (*epi*: upon) all these things put on charity (*agape*: divine love), which is the bond (*sundesmos*: adhesive, glue) of perfectness (*telios*: maturity).

This verse explains the importance of building in the Christian life. Through the Word of God, we add daily to the knowledge in our lives. Through praying in the Holy Spirit, we edify and build up ourselves on the foundation of our most holy faith. Second Peter 1:5–7 emphasizes the importance of building layer upon layer on the foundation of faith.

The final floor of our building — the penthouse — is divine love (*agape*). *Agape* love is the cement, the glue that binds us together. We are to strive for the unity of the faith (Ephesians 4:3) and this is accomplished through the production of divine love. Plato said, "Two things are always held together by a third thing." That "thing" is the agape love of God. The indicator of divine maturity in our lives is love.

Our goal in the Christian life is to grow up. This occurs through the intake and application of the Word of God. True divine love is the absence of mental sins toward others: anger, jealousy, bitterness, envy, unforgiveness, etc. Divine love is equal in its operation toward both the believer and the unbeliever. It is truly seeing others as God sees them. This is the love of God — it is the bond of maturity. The Greek word for "bond" is *sundesmos,* which describes a girdle that was used to hold clothing and utensils together.

E. The Peace of God

3:15 And let the peace of God rule in your hearts, to which also you were called in one body; and be thankful.

And let the peace (*eirene*) of God (*christos*: Christ) rule (*brabeuo*: be an umpire, governor) in your hearts, to the which also ye are called (*kaleoo*: received a call) in one body; and be (*ginomai*: become) ye thankful (plural: ones).

Ephesians 4:3 brings out that our mission is also to keep a bond of peace (*eirene*) as we strive for the unity of the Spirit. Love and peace work hand in hand. Peace in our hearts can become a guide (Romans 12:18, 14:19; Hebrews 12:14). The peace of God can act as umpire to help us make decisions. We can walk in peace in a world that is falling apart.

With peace in our hearts, we can truly become thankful ones. Thanksgiving on the outside begins with a heart of love and peace on the inside (1 Peter 2:9). Praise to God always begins with a grateful heart.

F. The Indwelling Word of Christ

3:16 Let the word of Christ dwell in you richly in all wisdom, teaching and admonishing one another in psalms and hymns and spiritual songs, singing with grace in your hearts to the Lord.

Let the word of Christ dwell (*enotkeo*: inhabit) in you richly (*pleusios*: to the point of saturation) in all wisdom (*sophia*: wisdom); teaching (*didasko*: to teach, to be a teacher, to impart instruction) and admonishing (*nouthoteo*: to exhort, warn) one another in psalms (*psalmas*: Old Testament psalms) and hymns (*humnos*: songs sung acapella) and spiritual songs (*ode*: songs that come from the Holy Spirit), singing with grace in your hearts to the Lord.

When the Word of God dwells richly in our hearts, to the point of saturation and overflowing, it will be manifested as worship and praise to the Lord. Next, the Word will manifest itself in admonition and instruction to other believers through the guidance of the Holy Spirit (Ephesians 5:18).

God has given us music not only to inspire, but also to teach the promises of God. Instruction can flow through us in teaching and songs of worship. The book of Psalms is our example. Although the music may be lost to us, the words remain intact. The teaching is the important part; the music is simply the vehicle to bring it to us. All of this comes through us from a heart that understands grace.

The Spirit and the Word want to do the same thing — glorify God. The Holy Spirit will use our voices as His instrument — as His vessel — if we will allow Him to do so.

G. Being a Doer of the Word

3:17 And whatever you do in word or deed, *do* all in the name of the Lord Jesus, giving thanks to God the Father through Him.

And whatsoever (*pan*: everything) ye do in word (*logos*: utterance) or deed, do all in the name of the Lord Jesus, giving thanks to God and the Father by him.

In the previous verses, the Word of God has been demonstrated through words of praise, worship, and instruction to others. Now it will display itself through our actions. Just as our words give thanks to God, so do our deeds. Everything we say and do is either a form of instruction to others or thanks to God. The Word dwelling in us richly becomes a witness to others. It causes us to be better wives (18), husbands (19), children (20), parents (21), employees (22–25), and bosses(4:1).

III. Establishment of the Christian Life (18–25)

Specific instructions are given to husbands, wives, and children as well as to employees and employers in these verses for practical living as a witness before our families and the world.

A. Family

3:18 ¶ Wives, submit to your own husbands, as is fitting in the Lord.

Wives (*gune*), submit (*hupotasso*: to place yourself) yourselves unto your own husbands, as it is fit (*anecho*: becoming, proper) in the Lord.

Instructions begin with the wife. She is the bearer of the children and the support of the husband in the family. She guides the family into the next generation, as she is responsible for the major upbringing of the children. She is to voluntarily submit herself to her husband.

This is not something the husband can command his wife to do. The husband is commanded to love and cherish his wife. By providing for her, he gives her a security to voluntarily submit herself to him.

This verse ends by simply telling us that it is God's plan that wives submit to their own husbands. There is no way around this command; God has no secondary plan. If God's plan is "fitting" to Him, then it is intended for success and not failure. It is also intended for our happiness and spiritual fulfillment, not our sorrow.

3:19 ¶ Husbands, love your wives and do not be bitter toward them.

Husbands (*aner*), love (*agape*: divine love) your wives, and be not bitter against them.

The love the husband has for his wife is the kind of love Jesus has for His church (Ephesians 5:25). This type of love is patient and kind and is willing to wait for change instead of demanding it and becoming angry when it does not come overnight.

A husband has a tendency to become angry when the rest of the family does not appreciate him for his financial contributions. He spends years in anger against the wife and the children and misses the best years of enjoyment. When a father or husband becomes angry, he abuses his authority. His example for love should be the Lord Jesus who never becomes bitter over His church. Though we may not respect or appreciate Him, He continues to love us.

3:20 ¶ Children, obey your parents in all things, for this is well pleasing to the Lord.

Children, obey (*hupakouo*: to hear, to place yourself under the sound of) your parents in all things (*panta*: every area): for this is well pleasing unto the Lord.

Wives are to submit and children are to obey. "Submit" means to place yourself under the sound of. When a wife submits herself to her own husband, it is called "fitting." When a child obeys his parents, it is called "well pleasing." God gives special commendation to those who submit and obey. No commendation was given to the husband for loving, because this is expected from the Lord. The honor goes to those who place themselves under the authority of others and under the sound of their voice. God also gives rewards to those who obey. Children who obey their parents receive a special promise from the Lord: long life and prosperity (Exodus 20:12, Ephesians 6:1–3). The areas in which children are to obey are "in the Lord" (Ephesians 6:1).

3:21 ¶ Fathers, do not provoke your children, lest they become discouraged.

Fathers (*pater*: parents), provoke not your children (*teknon*) to anger, lest they be discouraged (*atheumeo*: disheartened, despondent).

Anger comes in children when the parents tell them what to do, but give no instruction and lifestyle to back it up (Ephesians 6:4). The saying "Do what I say and not what I do" causes anger in children.

Children need to know that the Word of God is the authority behind your words and actions and that what directs your actions will also direct their actions. All of our proper deeds and lifestyles come from the Word of God. Parents have no excuse before God or their children for living a different type of lifestyle. When children are told what to do and not shown what to do, they become discouraged.

B. Employees

3:22 ¶ Bondservants, obey in all things your masters according to the flesh, not with eyeservice, as men-pleasers, but in sincerity of heart, fearing God.

Servants (*doulos*: a slave, a servant), obey (*upakouo*: to listen, to obey a command) in all things your masters (*kurios*: master, the Lord) according to the flesh; not with eyeservice (*ophthalmodouleia*: eye slaves, working only when boss is looking), as menpleasers; but in singleness of heart, fearing (*phobeo*: reverencing) God (*kurios*: masters, the Lord):

We have a play on words in this verse. The Greek word *kurios* is used twice, once for natural bosses on the earth and once for the Lord Jesus. We work for natural lords on this earth, but we only serve one Lord in heaven. Our work should be done in respect to those in authority with all reverence to the one Lord who sees everything we do. This is called singleness of heart. When we try to work both ends against the middle, we have a divided heart.

A Christian may try to get away with something with his earthly boss and think that God did not see. However, a Christian does not actually work for two opposing bosses, but two in unity. He may get away with something in the workplace, but never in life. Men may not see what a Christian does, but the Lord sees all.

Bosses only have authority over us in the natural — in "the flesh." They cannot dictate to us in spiritual matters or cause us to do things that contradict the Word of God. Promotion will come when we learn to please the Lord and do our jobs to the best of our abilities.

3:23 And whatever you do, do it heartily, as to the Lord and not to men,

And whatsoever ye do (*poieo*: to carry out, to execute), do (*ergazomai*: to work, labor, acquire) it heartily (*psuche*: from the soul), as to the Lord, and not unto men;

Working from the soul is a reference to a mind filled with the promises and stability of the Word. Believers do not necessarily make the best employees. It is mature believers who make the best employees. When a believer applies the same Word of God in his job and toward his boss as he does to believe God and have his needs met, he becomes a great employee and God will reward him.

3:24 knowing that from the Lord you will receive the reward of the inheritance; for you serve the Lord Christ.

Knowing that of (from) the Lord ye shall receive (*apolambano*: receive back) the reward of the inheritance: for ye serve the Lord Jesus Christ.

Serving others on the earth causes rewards to come in time as well as in eternity. Our inheritance does not begin when we are in heaven, but it begins on the earth as we receive rewards of the inheritance.

3:25 But he who does wrong will be repaid for what he has done, and there is no partiality.

The believer who does not do his job as unto the Lord and is lazy and irresponsible will receive discipline from the Lord. Just because you work around unbelievers is no excuse to loaf. God does not respect you more on the job than He does an unbeliever. When it comes to hard work, supporting your family, and being a model employee, God is no respecter of persons. If you are not working hard, do not be upset when the unbeliever is promoted and you are not. God does not owe you a promotion because you are His child. He is a rewarder of those who diligently seek Him.

Chapter Summary

Paul exhorts the Colossians to renew their minds by daily meditating on who they are in Christ and reminding them that their lives are hidden in Him. He also encourages them to put off their old fleshly man and its works, and to put on the new man, which is as easy as taking off old clothing and putting on new clothing.

Paul instructs the Colossians to walk in forgiveness and love toward one another. He also tells the Colossians that the goal of the Christian life should be to grow in maturity and that this maturity is the product of allowing divine love to operate in their lives.

Paul emphasizes the importance of the Colossians renewing their minds through meditating on the Word of God, and that as an outflow of a renewed mind, psalms, hymns, and spiritual songs should result which, in turn, serves as admonition and instruction toward others.

Finally, Paul exhorts husbands, wives, children, employees, and employers to demonstrate the Word of God by serving one another in excellence through being doers of the Word. He emphasized the fact that everything that is done in the Christian life should be done to the best of their ability as unto the Lord Himself.

4:1–18 Closing Exhortations, Instructions, and Greetings

The Challenge of Chapter Four

As we continue to grow in the knowledge of God's Word, our prayer lives should develop as should our thankfulness to God. We should mature in our walks, not only in our treatment of believers, but also in our witness before unbelievers.

I. Employers (1)

Paul encourages managers to treat those under their supervision fairly and without partiality.

4:1 ¶ Masters, give your bondservants what is just and fair, knowing that you also have a Master in heaven.

Masters (*kurios*: management), give (*parecho*: render from your own resources) unto your servants that which is just (fair) and equal (equitable); knowing that ye also have a Master in heaven.

Bosses are to treat their employees as the Lord treats them. The Lord treats every believer fairly and rewards without partiality (Ephesians 6:9). The Lord in heaven is the perfect master who never sleeps. His attention is always on us, and we cannot hide from Him. He always sees, not only our outward actions, but also the intentions of our heart. Our secret life is as public before the Lord as our outward life is before the world. Therefore, a natural boss should always remember he is accountable to his boss in heaven.

II. An Exhortation to Prayer (2–4)

Paul encourages the Colossian saints to make prayer their top priority and to include thanksgiving as a part of their prayer life.

A. Steadfast Prayer

4:2 ¶ Continue earnestly in prayer, being vigilant in it with thanksgiving;

Continue (be steadfast) in prayer (*proseuchomai*: face-to-face petition, intense prayer), and watch (be alert) in the same (at the same time) with thanksgiving;

Every believer who has been built up in the Word should be steadfast in prayer. "Steadfast" means we are to make prayer a top priority. Only mature believers are called on to be steadfast in prayer for those in ministry. Paul calls on the mature saints in Colosse to pray and be alert at the same time. We must remain alert because, while we are praying, the Holy Spirit speaks and gives us direction.

B. Prayer with Thanksgiving

Thanksgiving is also mentioned in verse 2 because it should accompany each prayer that we make (Philippians 4:6, 1 Thessalonians 5:16–18).

1. Thanksgiving is the outward demonstration of faith through the words of our mouth or the actions of our body.
2. Thanksgiving should be the mental attitude of every believer (Ephesians 5:20).
3. Thanksgiving is based on knowing God through His Word (Psalm 100:3–5, Colossians 2:7).
4. Thanksgiving is part of our priestly sacrifice (Psalm 107:22, 116:17; Amos 4:5, Hebrews 13:15).
5. Thanksgiving is a function of maturity (2 Corinthians 4:15, 9:10–11; Colossians 3:15).
6. Thanksgiving is related to prayer (Philippians 4:6).
7. Thanksgiving accompanies prayer for food (1 Timothy 4:3–5).
8. God is our object of thanksgiving (2 Corinthians 9:15).

C. Prayer for Open Doors of Opportunity

4:3 meanwhile praying also for us, that God would open to us a door for the word, to speak the mystery of Christ, for which I am also in chains,

The open door that Paul is praying for is a chance to preach the gospel and teach believers of the mystery doctrine and the uniqueness of the church age. For these open doors, Paul asks for prayer assistance from the church at Colosse. We should always pray for open doors:

1. Of communication (2 Corinthians 2:12, Colossians 4:3).

2. Of service (1 Corinthians 16:9).

3. Of regained fellowship (Revelation 3:20).

4. For blessings for mature believers (Revelation 3:8).

5. For the rapture (Revelation 4:1).

6. For the second advent (Psalm 24:7–8, Revelation 19:11).

7. Of salvation (John 10:9, Acts 14:27).

D. Prayer for Paul's Message to be in Simplicity

4:4 that I may make it manifest, as I ought to speak.

That I may make it manifest (*phanaroo*: clear), as I ought to speak (is my obligation).

Paul also wants the Colossian saints to pray for him so that he can make his teachings of the gospel simple and clear. This is probably difficult for Paul to do since he is such a teacher of the height, depth, and length of the Word of God. Making things simple is a matter of prayer for Paul. This is also the duty of each believer.

III. Living Wisely Before the World (5–6)

Paul explains to the Colossians the importance of living the Christian life wisely before the world, not only in word but especially in deed.

A. Our Deeds

4:5 ¶ Walk in wisdom toward those *who are* outside, redeeming the time.

Walk in wisdom (*sophia*: wisdom from the Word) toward them that are without (unbelievers), redeeming (buying back) the time.

The best witnesses are those who show their witness before talking their witness. This all goes back to letting the Word of Christ dwell in you richly (3:16–17). Our final goal is to be a witness to the unbeliever through our words and deeds (3:17). Witnessing should be the outward display of wisdom of the Word in our hearts (2 Timothy 3:16–17).

B. Our Words

4:6 ¶ Let your speech always *be* with grace, seasoned with salt, that you may know how you ought to answer each one.

Two things are brought out about our words when witnessing. Our words are to be gracious and our words are to be sprinkled with the Word of God. Salt represents the Word of God. We don't need to practice how to answer every man. As we are filled with God's Word and the Holy Spirit, we will know how to answer.

C. Salt

1. Salt is a preservative and a seasoning.

2. Eating salt with the king meant you had an allegiance to him. Salt makes the disagreeable agreeable.

3. Peace treaties were made by eating bread and salt together.

4. Eating salt was an expression of hospitality. When you ate salt together, even with an enemy, he could do you no physical harm while you were in his home.

5. As a judgment, Carthage was sown with salt by the Romans in 146 BC. It kept anything from growing after destruction.

6. Salt was not plentiful in the ancient world and, at times, was valued as gold. The Latin word for "salt" is *sal* from which the Romans derived *salarium* — salt money. Our word "salary" comes from this word; we "earn our salt" or are not "worth our salt."

7. Salt seasons food (Job 6:6–7). This is a type of the Word of God making life more enjoyable.

   a) Salt was put on some of the Levitical offerings (Leviticus 2:13).

   b) Sacrifices during the millennium will have salt (Ezekiel 43:24).

8. Used as judgment three ways in scripture:

   a) Personal: Lot's wife (Genesis 19:26).

   b) Temporal: Cities (Deuteronomy 29:23, Judges 9:45).

   c) Eternal: The Lake of Fire (Mark 9:48–49).

9. Believers are called salt.

   a) NaCl (sodium chloride).

b) Chlorine gas comes from the air (spirits). John 3:3 " . . . except ye be born of the Spirit."

c) Sodium is a chemical that comes from the ground and is black.

d) When sodium and chloride meet, a new substance is created (2 Corinthians 5:17).

e) The new substance can preserve.

10. Believers are the ones who preserve a nation (Matthew 5:13, Mark 9:50).

11. Salt stops growth in the soil. The salt that preserves also hinders (The believer who looses, also binds).

12. Unsaltiness is a type of reversionism and discipline (Luke 14:34–35).

13. Salt was used as an antiseptic for newborn babies (Ezekiel 16:4). This practice is still used among the Bedouins.

14. Salt is a type of the covenant between God and the believer (Numbers 13:5, 18:19).

IV. Final Greetings (7–18)

Paul sends greetings to the Colossian saints through and on behalf of his fellow brethren and bondservants of the Lord.

A. Tychicus

4:7 ¶ Tychicus, a beloved brother, faithful minister, and fellow servant in the Lord, will tell you all the news about me.

All my state (*tapanta*: All things concerning me) shall Tychicus declare unto you, who is a beloved (*agapetos*: beloved, dear) brother, and a faithful (*pistos*: trustworthy, sure, true) minister and fellowservant (*sundoulos*: servant with the same master) in the Lord:

Tychicus possesses three qualities that cause him to be a good minister. First, he is a "beloved brother." This indicates a good relationship with other ministers. Next, Paul mentions his faithfulness as a minister, which shows Tychicus's love for the people of God over whom he has been placed. Finally, he is said to be a "fellowservant." This indicates his love for and relationship with the Lord.

1. The first mention of Tychicus is as he first joined Paul on his third missionary journey (Acts 20:4)

2. Tychicus, along with Trophimus, was from Asia Minor.

3. While Trophimus went to Jerusalem with Paul, Tychicus remained in Asia (Acts 20:15, 28).

4. Tychicus was with Paul during the first imprisonment (Ephesians 6:21–22, Colossians 4:7).

5. Tychicus is mentioned again in Titus 3:12.

6. Each time his name is mentioned in the epistles, Tychicus is being sent by Paul to bring word of his well-being to the churches and report back to Paul of the conditions in each area (Colossians 4:8, 2 Timothy 4:12).

4:8 I am sending him to you for this very purpose, that he may know your circumstances and comfort your hearts,

Tychicus will come to Colosse to bring news of Paul, and then return to Paul to bring news of the condition of Colosse.

B. Onesimus

4:9 with Onesimus, a faithful and beloved brother, who is *one* of you. They will make known to you all things which *are happening* here.

With Onesimus, a faithful and beloved brother, who is one of you. They shall make known unto you all things which are done here.

Onesimus was a runaway slave who belonged to Philemon. The church at Colosse probably met in the home of Philemon and knew about the young man, Onesimus, who had stolen money from his master and fled to Rome. While in Rome he ran out of money and was put in prison with Paul. Paul won him to the Lord and Onesimus returned to Philemon's home and to the church. The letter written to Philemon is Paul's request for him to forgive Onesimus and accept him back as a brother in the Lord.

C. Aristarchus

4:10 ¶ Aristarchus my fellow prisoner greets you, with Mark the cousin of Barnabas (about whom you received instructions: if he comes to you, welcome him),

Aristarchus my fellowprisoner saluteth you . . .

Aristarcus joined Paul on his third missionary journey and was with Paul during the revival in Ephesus. A riot broke out under Dimetrius, and Aristarchus was almost killed by the crowd who dragged him into the streets while pursuing Paul (Acts 19:29). After this he accompanied Paul to Greece and Asia (Acts 20:4) and finally to Rome where he stayed with Paul in prison (Acts 27:2, Colossians 4:10, Philemon 24).

D. Marcus

. . . and Marcus, sister's son to Barnabas (touching whom ye received commandments: if he come unto you, receive him ;)

Marcus is John Mark, the nephew of Barnabas. He accompanied Paul and Barnabas on their first missionary journey (Acts 12:25, 13:5). He deserted them and became the object of great dissension causing the eventual breakup of Paul and Barnabas as a team (Acts 15:36–39). Mark eventually became a great minister and Paul received him as such (2 Timothy 4:11).

E. Justus

4:11 and Jesus who is called Justus. These *are my* only fellow workers for the kingdom of God who are of the circumcision; they have proved to be a comfort to me.

This is the only mention of Justus, a Jewish minister with Paul in prison. He, along with the others in prison, was there to encourage Paul.

F. Epaphras

4:12 ¶ Epaphras, who is *one* of you, a bondservant of Christ, greets you, always laboring fervently for you in prayers, that you may stand perfect and complete in all the will of God.

Epaphras, who is one of you, a servant of Christ, saluteth you, always labouring fervently for you in prayers, that ye may stand perfect (*telios*: mature) and complete (*pleroo*: perfect middle: having been made complete) in all the will of God.

Epaphras, like Onesimus, is from the area of Colosse. He is the pastor of the church at Colosse and is now visiting Paul in prison. Paul commends him on his love for the people of the church. Epaphras displays his love for the people by teaching them of the will of God, making them complete in the Word, so they can stand mature.

This is the purpose of the local church and the pastor. There should not be an area in the Word that the pastor cannot teach the people. He must train his people in all the Word of God so they may know all of God's will for this dispensation and for their own personal lives and callings.

Epaphras prayed, not for his teaching ability or the anointing of the Holy Spirit on his sermons, but for the people to grow in all of the will of God. His prayers were for the people to listen, retain, and grow through the sermons he preached.

4:13 For I bear him witness that he has a great zeal for you, and those who are in Laodicea, and those in Hierapolis.

Epaphras was concerned, not only for his church and area, but he was concerned for all of the surrounding areas and churches. He was not in competition with them, but was also praying for them to grow in all of the will of God.

G. Luke

4:14 Luke the beloved physician and Demas greet you.

Luke, the beloved physician . . .

Luke is mentioned as being with Paul on many occasions. He is the writer of the book of Luke and also Acts. He is faithful to Paul as a comforter, traveling companion, and reporter of the ministry of Paul.

H. Demas

. . . and Demas, greet you.

Demas has been with Paul on occasion as a fellow laborer (Philemon 24). He later deserts Paul for the things of the world (2 Timothy 4:10).

I. Nymphas

4:15 Greet the brethren who are in Laodicea, and Nymphas and the church that is in his house.

Nymphas was a prominent Christian and had opened his home to the church at Laodicea for assembly and worship.

4:16 ¶ Now when this epistle is read among you, see that it is read also in the church of the Laodiceans, and that you likewise read the *epistle* from Laodicea.

Paul is already concerned about the church at Laodicea. They are not advancing like Paul would like for them to, and they do not seem to desire the Word in the same way as the church at Colosse. This is the church John wrote to and declared they were neither hot or cold and were too wrapped up in material possessions (Revelations 3:14–22). One of the major problems is mentioned in the next verse; the pastor, Archippus is not taking the ministry seriously.

J. Archippus

4:17 And say to Archippus, "Take heed to the ministry which you have received in the Lord, that you may fulfill it."

And say to Archippus, Take heed to the ministry which thou hast received in the Lord, that thou fulfil (*pleroo*: to make full, complete) it.

Archippus (master horseman), was the pastor at Laodicea. He did not have the love for the people, the Word, and the Lord as Epaphras did. He, like Timothy, was not making "full proof of his ministry." Words of admonition caused Timothy to turn around but apparently did not change Archippus. Paul calls Archippus a "fellow soldier" in Philemon 2. There is no record of what happened to Archippus.

4:18 This salutation by my own hand—Paul. Remember my chains. Grace *be* with you. Amen.

Chapter Summary

Paul exhorts employers (masters) to treat their employees (servants) fairly and reminds them that God is the ultimate boss over every man's life.

Paul also encourages the Colossian saints to be faithful in prayer, to be alert for the direction of the Holy Spirit. He reminds them that prayer should always be accompanied by thanksgiving. He also asks the Colossians to pray a door of utterance be opened for him to preach and teach the gospel. He also instructs the Colossians to walk as a witness before the world in both word and deed.

Paul concludes this book by sending greetings to the Church at Colosse from and through a number of fellow laborers for the Lord.

Reference Book List

Barclay, William. 1976. *New Testament Words*. Westminster: John Knox Press.

Jamison, Robert, David Brown, and A.R. Fausset. 1997. *A Commentary on the Old and New Testaments* (3 Volume Set). Peabody, MA: Hendrickson Publishers.

Strong, James H. 1980. *Strong's Exhaustive Concordance of the Bible*, 15th ed. Nashville, TN: Abingdon Press.

Strong, James, and Joseph Thayer. 1995. *Thayers Greek-English Lexicon of the New Testament: Coded with Strong's Concordance Numbers*. Peabody, MA: Hendrickson Publishers.

Unger, Merrill. 1996. *Vine's Complete Expository Dictionary of Old and New Testament Words: With Topical Index*. Nashville, TN: Thomas Nelson.

Vincent, Marvin R. 1985. *Vincent Word Studies in the New Testament* (4 Volume Set). Peabody, MA: Hendrickson Publishers.

Wuest, Kenneth. 1980. *Word Studies from the Greek New Testament,* 2nd ed. (4 Volume Set). Grand Rapids: MI: William B. Eerdmans Publishing Company.

Zodhiates, Spiros, 1991. *The Complete Word Study New Testatment* (Word Study Series). Chatanooga, TN: AMG Publishers.

The writings of Arthur W. Pink.

The writings and audio recordings of Donald Grey Barnhouse.

Meet Bob Yandian

From 1980 to 2013, Bob Yandian was the pastor of Grace Church in his hometown of Tulsa, Oklahoma. After 33 years, he left the church to his son, Robb, with a strong and vibrant congregation. During those years, he raised up and sent out hundreds of ministers to churches and missions organizations in the United States and around the world. He has authored over thirty books and established a worldwide ministry to pastors and ministers.

He is widely acknowledged as one of the most knowledgeable Bible teachers of this generation. His practical insight and wisdom into the Word of God has helped countless people around the world to live successfully in every area of the daily Christian life.

Bob attended Southwestern College and is also a graduate of Trinity Bible College. He has served as both instructor and dean of instructors at Rhema Bible College in Broken Arrow, Oklahoma.

Bob has traveled extensively throughout the United States and internationally, taking his powerful and easy to apply teachings that bring stability and hope to hungry hearts everywhere. He is called "a pastor to pastors."

Bob and his wife, Loretta, have been married for over forty years, are parents of two married children, and have five grandchildren. Bob and Loretta Yandian reside in Tulsa, Oklahoma.

Contact Bob Yandian Ministries

Email: bym@bobyandian.com

Phone:

(918) 250-2207

Mailing Address:

Bob Yandian Ministries

PO Box 55236

Tulsa, OK 74155

www.bobyandian.com

PRAYER OF SALVATION

God loves you — no matter who you are, no matter what your past. God loves you so much that He gave His one and only begotten Son for you. The Bible tells us that ". . . whoever believes in him shall not perish but have eternal life" (John 3:16 NIV). Jesus laid down His life and rose again so that we could spend eternity with Him and experience His absolute best on earth. If you would like to receive Jesus into your life, say the following prayer out loud and mean it in your heart.

Heavenly Father, I come to You admitting that I am a sinner. Right now, I choose to turn away from sin, and I ask You to cleanse me of all unrighteousness. I believe that Your Son, Jesus, died on the cross to take away my sins. I also believe that He rose again from the dead so that I might be forgiven of my sins and made righteous through faith in Him. I call upon the name of Jesus Christ to be the Savior and Lord of my life. Jesus, I choose to follow You and ask that You fill me with the power of the Holy Spirit. I declare that, right now, I am a child of God. I am free from sin and full of the righteousness of God. I am saved in Jesus's name. Amen.

If you prayed this prayer to receive Jesus Christ as your Savior for the first time, please contact us to receive a free book:

www.harrisonhouse.com
Harrison House
PO Box 35035
Tulsa, Oklahoma 74153

Fast. Easy.
Convenient.

For the latest Harrison House product information and author news, look no further than your computer. All the details on our powerful, life-changing products are just a click away. New releases, email subscriptions, testimonies, monthly specials — find them all in one place. Visit harrisonhouse.com today!

harrisonhouse.com

Made in the USA
Middletown, DE
10 April 2019